GHOSTS 2
CAUGHT ON FILM

PHOTOGRAPHS OF THE UNEXPLAINED

JIM EATON

A DAVID & CHARLES BOOK
Copyright © David & Charles Limited 2009

David & Charles is an F+W Media Inc. company
4700 East Galbraith Road
Cincinnati, OH 45236

First published in the UK in 2009
First published in the US in 2009

Text copyright © Jim Eaton 2009
Photographs copyright © see page 159

Jim Eaton has asserted his right to be identified as author of this work in
accordance with the Copyright, Designs and Patents Act, 1988.

A catalogue record for this book is available from the British Library.

ISBN-13: 978-0-7153-3202-3 hardback
ISBN-10: 0-7153-3202-3 hardback

Printed in China by SNP Leefung
for David & Charles
Brunel House, Newton Abbot, Devon

Commissioning Editor: Neil Baber
Editorial Manager: Emily Pitcher
Editor: Verity Muir
Proofreader: Cheryl Brown
Senior Designer: Jodie Lystor
Production Controller: Kelly Smith

Visit our website at www.davidandcharles.co.uk

David & Charles books are available from all good bookshops; alternatively you
can contact our Orderline on 0870 9908222 or write to us at FREEPOST EX2
110, D&C Direct, Newton Abbot, TQ12 4ZZ (no stamp required UK only); US
customers call 800-289-0963 and Canadian customers call 800-840-5220.

Contents

GHOSTS 2
CAUGHT ON FILM

INTRODUCTION

This book is about photographic evidence – the kind of evidence that may help to prove that ghosts exist. Visual evidence, if it can be obtained, is always so much more compelling than any second-hand report or story. Of course most of the pictures that apparently show the supernatural have perfectly natural explanations, but there are some that I feel are worthy of closer inspection. It's certainly not an exact science but I hope that perhaps one day a photograph *will* provide irrefutable proof, and even that cameras of the future will be developed that are capable of routinely photographing the supernatural. That's why I study photos of supernatural phenomena and always try to keep an open mind. The more photos that we study, the more we are likely to learn.

Ghost stories have been told for thousands of years and there are many people who are prepared to swear, as a result of their personal experiences, that ghosts exist. But there is, as yet, no unequivocal proof. No one has produced evidence that will stand up to enquiry under controlled conditions that can be measured and duplicated. The famous paranormal investigator

and sceptic James Randi has even offered a $1million reward for anyone 'who can show, under proper observing conditions, evidence of any paranormal, supernatural, or occult power or event', but the prize remains unclaimed.

It has always been my belief that photos offer the best chance of finding proof – seeing is believing, after all. With that in mind I started Ghoststudy.com in 1999. It has since become the largest free ghost photo website on the internet and has given me the opportunity to study many thousands of anomolous photographs. Investigating the images is a process of illimination: ruling out optical illusions, photo manipulation, smoke or any of the other common causes of strange appeareances on

photographs. What is then left may be worthy of our further consideration. I have also discovered that photographs are a great way of raising the profile of the field of ghost hunting. Their immediacy draws in the crowds and people can judge the evidence for themselves, rather than having to take someone else's word.

Ghost hunting, for some, is a full-time profession. Television shows such as *Ghost Hunters* (TAPS), *Most Haunted* and *Ghost Hunters International* cater for a growing interest in paranormal activity. Paranormal investigators are dedicated individuals who travel widely to research supernatural phenomena. They work strange, long hours monitoring locations suspected of being haunted. They run hundreds of feet of

cable, monitoring several rooms at once, using
state-of-the-art equipment. Yet people going
about their everyday business have just as much
chance of capturing ghost images using digital
and mobile phone cameras. In fact many ghost
images have gone unnoticed for years between
the pages of family photo albums.

I hope you enjoy this collection of some of the
most interesting images I have come across. I
invite you to look through and decide for yourself:
is there evidence here of ghosts caught on film?
Check out your photo albums as well to see if
any ghostly images are lurking there and, most
importantly, grab your camera and start taking
more pictures. I can't wait to see what you get!
                                    – Jim Eaton

GHOSTLY FIGURES

Ghostly figures can encompass many types of supernatural beings, and the following list describes the most often-seen types:

Apparition: when an invisible being becomes visible.

Ghost: the spirit of a person who has died but lingers on in our plane of existence.

Phantom: a being that does not exist physically but which can, on occasion, be seen, heard and felt.

Spectre: a disembodied being...a ghost of sorts.

Spirit: the soul or life force of a human being.

Wraith: the apparition of a person living or thought to be alive and supposed to appear around the time of his death.

Bogeyman: an entity that terrorizes and is feared.

Shadow being: an apparition that displays as either a dark mass or a shadowy human form.

Orb or spirit globules: believed by many to be the soul or spirit of someone who has passed on from this life.

Ghost hunters spend their lives in search of these ghostly figures. They stay up all night in haunted houses, cemeteries, and other dark and creepy places, all in the hope of getting that one piece of evidence that will prove the existence of these supernatural beings. They invest their time and money to buy increasingly sophisticated and expensive equipment. They hope to circulate among the unseen and to rub shoulders (so to speak) with disembodied souls. And yet, interestingly, most of the ghost images in this chapter were taken by chance, by people going about their everyday business, using digital and mobile phone cameras. We're sure a ghost was the last thing the photographers expected to see in their pictures.

Ghostly figures are some of the most interesting images caught on film because they present themselves in a near human form. In this chapter there are photos of ghostly figures appearing in a truck, a church, a car, cemeteries, a cathedral, a haunted house, by the water's edge, and going through a door.

Officer Shoots Ghost

Roy, a Californian law enforcement officer, is a keen amateur photographer in his free time. Out taking pictures in his local area one day, he came across this old, abandoned truck on Honey Run Road in Chico – the perfect subject for a photo shoot.

Later when Roy downloaded the photographs he was amazed to see a man in the passenger seat of the truck looking straight at the camera – and clearly visible in this picture. Roy swears that there was nobody in or around the truck at the time he took these photographs. If this is the case, can we entertain the possibility that the vehicle is haunted? Is this, perhaps, an earthbound ghost going about his business?

'Roy swears that there was nobody in or around the truck at the time...'

Boy Chasing Orb

This photograph was taken by Jay, the father of the boy in the picture. He snapped the shot as his son dashed around in pursuit of some imaginary object. To the family's surprise, the resulting photograph revealed that their son's innocent chasing game had a more sinister purpose. An orb (believed by many to be the soul or spirit of someone who has passed on from this life) is clearly visible in the boy's path and the toddler appears to be chasing it.

A great many pictures of orbs that are taken with digital cameras turn out to be nothing more than dust or other airborne particles settling on or near the camera lens. Determining a true orb is no easy matter. The typical characteristics of a genuine orb or 'spirit globule' (as they are also known) is a misty or hazy ball, often stretched or elongated that appears to be in motion. This photograph seems to meet this criteria.

'their son's innocent chasing game had a more sinister purpose...'

Ghostly Cemetery Visit

A young family have just completed a visit to the cemetery to pay their respects to a loved one who has passed on. Before returning home, the doting father takes the opportunity to take a snap of the baby. But when the film is developed, what the young couple see in the photograph makes them vow never to return to the cemetery again...beyond the window two shroud-wrapped spectres can be seen making their way towards the car door.

Very often anomalies that appear on glass are the result of reflections and shadows, however this well-known image has stumped the many people who have examined it, for it does indeed appear that two hooded figures are just beyond the car door. It seems unlikely that this is a reflection of something inside the car, and although photo manipulation cannot be completely ruled out it is improbable, as the picture was taken in the late 1990s when such technology was less widespread. It's an intriguing image. Some people report seeing up to five ghostly images in the window. How many do you see?

'some people report seeing up to five ghostly images in the window...'

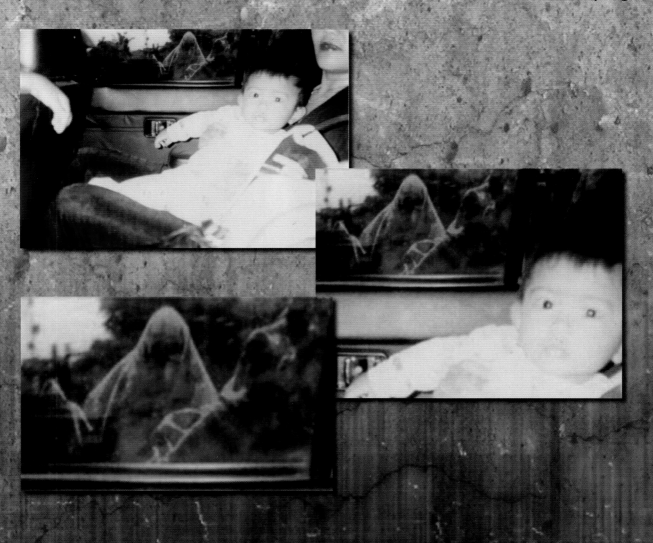

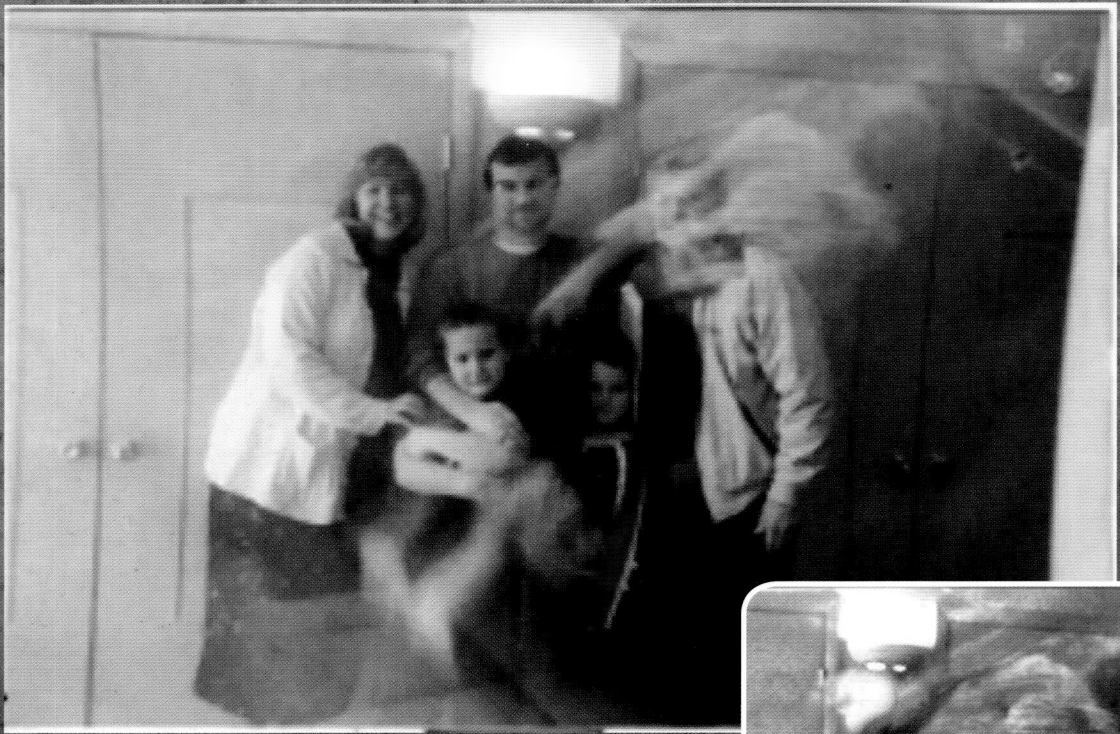

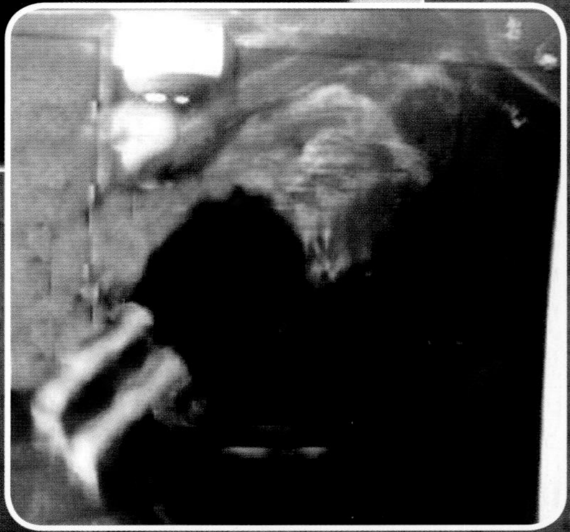

Floating Lost Soul

This incredibly creepy photo appears to show a floating lost soul eager to make its presence known on film. The picture was taken in a church in southwest Ohio and the only people present in the building were the five people who appear in the photo and the photographer. If this really is evidence of a lost soul caught on camera, we can only wonder what message the apparition was attempting to convey. Could it be that this person died of suspicious circumstances, or has he some unfinished business, and is it significant that this image was taken in a church?

According to the photographer, the film was brand new and was loaded into the camera just before the picture was taken. The entire roll was used up on the same day which makes the explanation of double exposure unlikely. The whitish haze is characteristic of an image shot through a reflective surface, but why would such a picture be taken through a sheet of glass or a window? If this picture really was the first frame on the film it is possible that light may have leaked onto the film while it was being loaded. Whatever the explanation, you can't deny the obvious presence of a ghostly body floating across the photo.

'Could it be that this person died of suspicious circumstances...'

It's Behind You

Despite this being such a famous ghost photo, its owner and its origins remain a mystery. This version has been circulating on the internet for the last ten years and has been cropped so that the viewer's attention is focused on the ghostly figure in the background. It's unfortunate that we don't have the complete photograph or more details about it as there are still so many unanswered questions. Who are the couple in the picture? Where was it taken? Could someone have recently died there?

The composition and clarity of a picture help to support claims of the supernatural and quite often we can even establish a cause for a sighting based on the circumstances reported by those present. In this case however, we have almost nothing to go on. We can establish that the photo is at least ten years old (and by the looks of it, much older) and that therefore photo manipulation is unlikely. Beyond that we can only admire an impressive photo of what appears to be a full-bodied apparition and hope that at some point we may discover more about the ghostly presence caught here.

'Could someone have recently died there?...'

Gravestone Appearance

A tourist to Guadalajara, Mexico, was enjoying a tour of the city's oldest and most haunted cemetery. One of the many fascinating stories told by the tour guide was at the final resting place of Englishwoman Jean Young Johnson. Jean had travelled with her husband to Guadalajara where they had settled and made their fortune. When Jean died in 1840, the locals left tokens at her grave as a mark of their respect, and many reported that their businesses prospered soon afterwards. Visitors continue to leave keepsakes at Jean's graveside in the hope of financial success, and the tourist used his mobile phone (which didn't have a flash) to take a picture of the gift-laden grave to remind him of this intriguing story.

'He was shocked to see a face at the top of the headstone...'

As the tour came to an end, the tour guide mentioned how visitors had often unexpectedly captured ghosts in their photos of the cemetery. Curious to see if he too had been lucky enough to catch an elusive spirit, the tourist looked closely at the picture he had just taken and was shocked to see a face at the top of the headstone. He passed around his camera phone in disbelief and the crowd were amazed at what they saw. As yet no one has been able to explain the picture. We know that the glowing face is not the effect of a camera flash, so perhaps it's the spirit of Jean Young Johnson after all.

Creature by the Water's Edge

While visiting his cousin in Hawaii, Arjun captured this unusual photo of what he calls 'the thing'. While others in his family went off to swim, Arjun decided to go out on his own and take a few scenic photographs. Equipped with just his camera, he went in search of a place that his cousin had shown him earlier that day. When he found the location he caught sight of an image that will be etched in his mind for the rest of his life.

To his alarm, he noticed something across the stream that quickly moved away from a tree and then straightened up and walked towards the water. According to Arjun, it was a black figure that resembled a human form but was definitely not a human being. Even though he was scared to death, he managed to take this quick shot of the shadow being before he scarpered off in a panic.

'He caught sight of an image that will be etched in his mind for the rest of his life...'

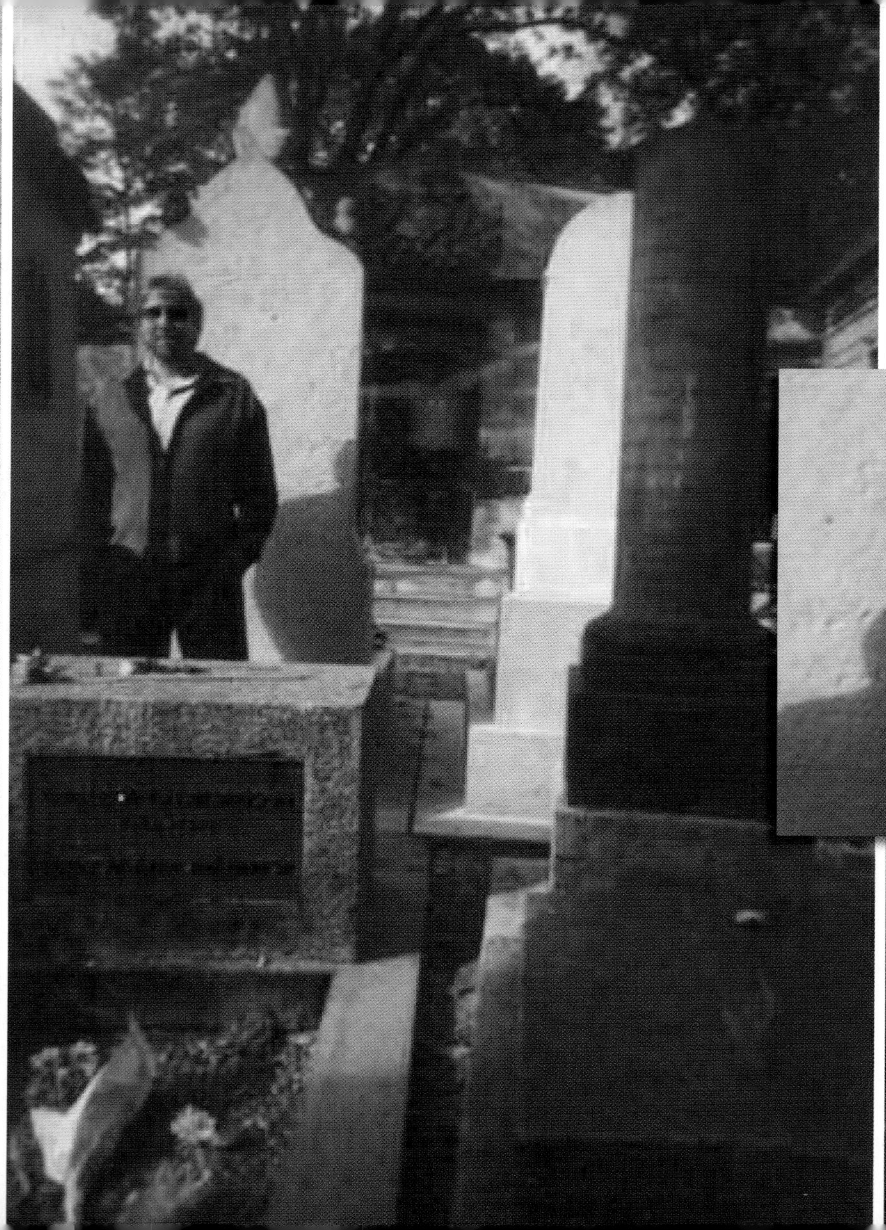

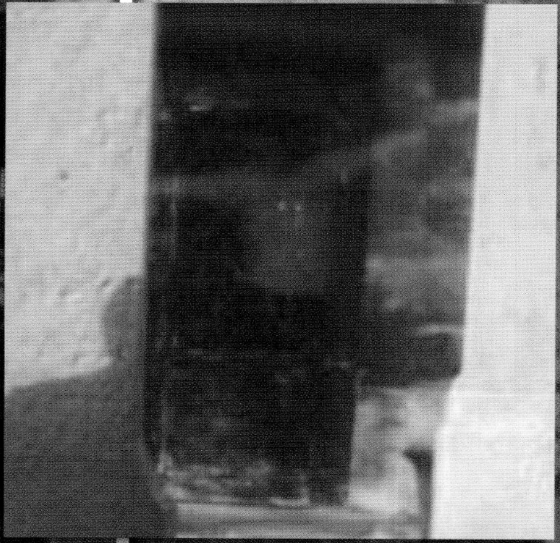

Jim Morrison's Ghost

The ghost in this picture is believed to be that of former lead singer of The Doors, Jim Morrison. The photograph was taken at Père Lachaise cemetery, the largest cemetery in Paris, France and in the foreground is Brett Meisner, a rock historian and huge Doors' fan. Brett visited the Morrison grave in 1997 like many hundreds of fans do each year, but it wasn't until 2002 that the iconic image of Jim Morrison standing in the background was brought to his attention by his assistant. Once word spread across the internet of the now notorious Morrison ghost photograph both the picture and negative were sent to various paranormal groups for analysis. Researchers were baffled by the image and deemed it 'unexplainable'.

Most of people seem to believe that this is an apparition of the famous singer himself; however, although crowds of people were there that day there are no reports of anyone else capturing a similar image. Some people put it down to a trick of the light, while others allude to the possibility of image manipulation. Meisner is currently trying to find a private and reputable organization to donate the photo and negative to because of the amount of unwanted attention he has received due to the popularity of the picture. So far he has no takers.

'Researchers were baffled by the image and deemed it 'unexplainable'...'

Stairway to Heaven

Imagine that you are investigating an old, abandoned house and suddenly you see a brightly glowing apparition coming up the stairs towards you, getting closer and closer – what would you do? Would fear take over and make you run for your life, or would you do as Tom did and take a picture!

Tom reports that he was standing in a bedroom doorway at the top of the stairs when he looked down and saw a huge glowing entity moving towards him. He waited until it reached the top of the staircase before taking a picture and by that point it had begun to fade and disappear. Two of Tom's fellow investigators were in the next room at the time and they reported a tremendous 'spike' in EMF (electromagnetic field) readings directly after the photo was taken. This was astounding, particularly as there were no other readings during the investigation, neither during the preliminary walk-through the day before, nor the night.

'He saw a huge glowing entity moving up the stairs towards him...'

Tom took the picture with a 35mm Pentax A300 with ISP 200 film and he used a flash. His colleague Greg reports that there was nothing reflective behind the bright image – the window was boarded up and the glass panes had been removed long before. According to Tom, a full analysis of the negative by Kodak Laboratories is planned in the hope that it may explain this mysterious blue figure.

Ghost at the Door

Camcorders are a useful tool for picking up traces of the afterlife, as John's story demonstrates. After developing a plan to capture ghosts on film, John set up a camcorder in his house and began a routine regiment of video-taping the early morning hours.

John had suffered months of nocturnal torment and thought that he was going insane when he heard whispering voices and doors violently banging shut. Even his dog would refuse to go downstairs at night and when forced, it would often scratch and bite at the door to get outside quickly. For his own sanity, John knew that he had to prove to himself and to others that this wasn't all in his mind and that something out of the ordinary was happening. Almost immediately he began to capture orbs and hear voices calling his name on the video tape. However, the biggest surprise was when he captured the ghostly image of what appears to be a man on the video. It wasn't obvious at first but when John slowed the tape down the figure could be clearly seen, and he could at last prove to the world that his suspicions had been confirmed and that he was indeed being haunted.

'he heard whispering voices and doors violently banging shut...'

Spirits in the Cathedral

What better place for spirits to appear than in the atmospheric surroundings of a holy house? The photographer, a tourist visiting the cathedral, appears to have captured a ghost family in this image – a parent with a small child (and is that a second child seated on the parent's lap?). The tourist claims that just seconds before he was sitting in the very same spot, having just got up to take the picture.

So is this picture evidence of an afterlife? There are, of course, several possibilities to explain this supernatural visitation. Perhaps the photographer was so overawed by his subject that he simply did not notice others in the area? And if this were the case, the movement made by a child running around could create this ghostly transparent affect. Yet how do we explain this same affect for the seated figures? Other theories could be offered – a slow shutter speed or photo manipulation for example – and yet we can never really know for sure, and you will have to decide for yourself what you believe.

'is this picture evidence of an afterlife?'

Cemetery Ghost Girl

After receiving a digital camera for his birthday, ghost enthusiast James and his wife took the new camera to a local cemetery to see if they could catch anything on film. They were reluctant to walk into the cemetery late at night, so they took the pictures from a nearby road. Although they didn't see or hear anything that night, what showed up in the picture startled them a greatly. The image of what appears to be a young girl in grey was captured walking across the cemetery in great haste. James and his wife swear that there were no other people there and that the cemetery was closed.

Astonished by what they had caught on camera, the couple returned the next day to investigate the scene in daylight. According to James' calculations, the size of the girl matched the size of the headstones, which would make the girl approximately 2ft (60cm) tall and probably no more than a few years old. Why, you have to ask yourself, would a girl – a child – be wandering about the premises of closed cemetery last thing at night?

'Although they didn't see or hear anything that night, what showed up in the picture startled them greatly...'

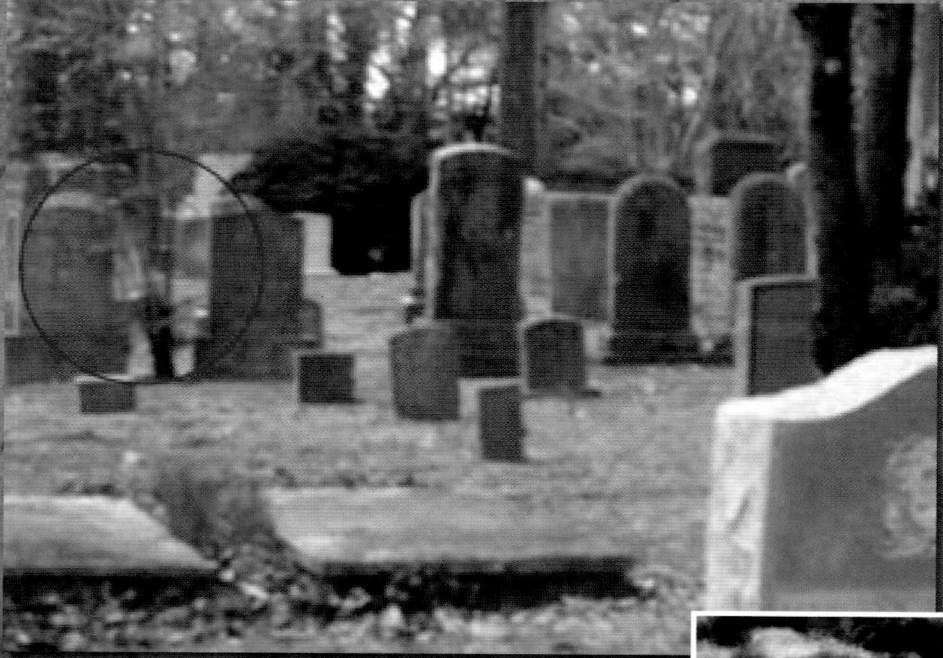

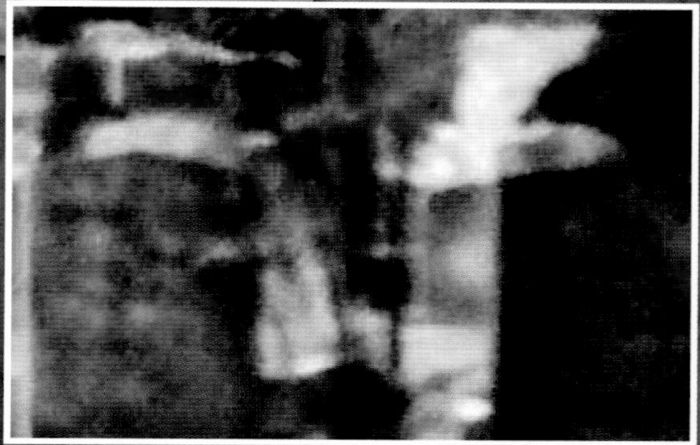

Girl Hugging Gravestone

This photo was first taken by Pete who was visiting a friend's grave at Virginia State Cemetery. Pete was inspired by the tranquility of the setting to take some photographs. After closely inspecting his developed pictures he discovered the image of a young girl who appears to be suspended in midair and embracing a large headstone. Is this the vision of a 'ghost girl' longing to be with the person who is buried there?

Of course we can't discount the possibility of this being a real person with the distance between photographer and subject causing the obscurity, but if this were the case surely Pete would have noticed the girl at the time the picture was taken. All we can do now is speculate.

'he discovered the image of a young girl...suspended in midair and embracing a large headstone...'

ETHEREAL PRESENCES

he photos in this chapter are dedicated
those supernatural beings that are misty,
porous, airy, sheer or transparent – in short,
hereal beings. As such they are often able to
enetrate solid objects such as doors and walls.
hereal beings are said to be made up of a
ghly refined tissue or substance that makes
em extremely difficult to capture on film.
ngels and guardians and other such spirits
ould fit into this category. Many believe that
hen we die, the spirit world is opened up to
and we have only to move in that direction.
owever for various reasons – unfinished

business or a strong attachment to someone
living – some stay behind and these are what
are known as ghosts. The tissue of a ghost is less
refined than that of a spirit and that means that
we are more likely to capture ghosts on film.

It's also possible that other paranormal
phenomena can appear as ethereal presences:

Astral traveller: in this instance the ghost
is actually a living person whose spirit has
separated from the physical body. It is then able
to travel in a separate dimension known as the

astral plane, and the astral traveller may then be seen by the living. For those interested in astral travel/projection, try the Monroe Method as a good starting point.

Residual haunting: this is where one experiences the energy rather than a ghost of someone who may have passed away as a result of traumatic events. For example if someone had been locked in a room and tortured there for a long period of time, their distress may have imprinted itself in the surroundings, and this may be played back like a recorded message.

Poltergeist: it is now believed that these have nothing to do with ghosts or spirits but are types of haunting phenomena – noisy rapping or banging on walls, electrical disturbances and objects moving or being thrown as if by some invisible force produced by subconscious psychokinesis generated by an individual, usually a girl 12 years or older. The individual is usually under emotional or psychological stress.

An Apparition of the Virgin Mary?

Two young girls claim to have captured this startling image of the Virgin Mary with their digital camera. The 12 year old girl who took the picture was staying at a cabin in Winthrop, Washington, USA with her family and a 15 year old friend. It was Christmas 2007 and she had just received a brand new camera as a gift. She and her friend decided to go outside to take some pictures in the snow. When this image appeared in the LCD screen, the girls began to feel uncomfortable in the eerie silence of their surroundings, so they hurried back to the cabin for safety. After uploading the pictures onto the computer they were able to see the image in full size, which only confirmed what they had viewed earlier in the camera's LCD screen — the vision of a woman.

The picture is so startling because of the amount of detail can be seen in the woman's hair and hood. Some even suggest that she is holding a baby. However, if you consider that it was cold and snowing and that the chilling temperatures can create visible exhaled breath, then we may be able to explain the occurrence of the image. Yet considering the amount of detail in the supposed exhalation, we can almost certainly rule this possibility out.

'The girls began to feel uncomfortable in the eerie silence of their surroundings...'.

Sacred Grounds' Guardian

The Sedona desert, south Arizona, is an area of breathtaking beauty, famous for its stunning red sandstone formations and well known for its psychic energies, spiritual pursuits and energy vortices. Before Europeans settled here about 500 years ago, the area had been sacred to aboriginal people since prehistoric times. It is not surprising therefore that this locality has had its fair share of supernatural sightings, from UFOs to ghosts.

These amazing pictures were taken in the heart of the desert, well off the beaten track, although unfortunately the photographer is unable to confirm the exact location. The images show a ghostly figure in what appears to be an ancient dwelling, standing upright in one and leaning over in the other. Is it an ancient being making spiritual repairs to its sacred home? Or perhaps the apparition is rising in defence of these sacred grounds? An analysis of the photographs cannot completely rule out explanations such as lens smudge, glare or photo manipulation; however, you must agree with the photographer when he says that on seeing this he felt the hair rise on his neck.

'Is it an ancient being making spiritual repairs to its sacred home?'

Phantom Dreams

It is widely accepted that ghosts can make their appearance in the form of ectoplasm or ectoplasmic-mist (ectomist) – a supernatural viscous substance once commonly seen exuding from the body of a medium during a spiritual trance and increasingly captured today by amateur photographers the world over.

This particular photo has been on the web for many years and it never ceases to amaze those who view it. The photographer had bought a new digital camera and was experimenting with it, taking pictures all over the house, including this shot of his brother fast asleep in his bedroom. Once the picture had revealed itself on the LCD screen, he was shocked to see a mysterious swirling vapour lay alongside his brother's sleeping form. There may be numerous explanations for the mist, such as common vapour or steam or smoke; but after discovering the ghostly presence on the picture the photographer became fearful of what might be dwelling in the house, and with such a startling image, who can blame him?

'A mysterious swirling vapour lay alongside his brother's form...'

Guardian Angel

In November 1998, 58 year old Rose Benvenuto was returning home late one evening when suddenly a stray dog ran across the path of her car causing her to swerve dramatically to avoid hitting it. This photograph was taken shortly after the road accident by fire department personnel called to the scene. In the background are the mangled remains of the victim's car and in the foreground a glowing figure appears to be taking its leave of the scene.

It may surprise you to learn that, thankfully, Rose survived the crash; in fact she was taken to hospital with only a minor arm injury. So if the ghostly apparition in this photo is not the driver's departing spirit, what can its explanation be? The photograph was one of several taken by Sharon Boo, photographer with the Pawling Fire Department, New York, USA. It is standard practice to photograph car accidents from every different angle, however only one of her pictures captured this strange figure. It resembles human form and size and even appears to have wings. Could this be photographic evidence of a guardian angel? Rose certainly believes that the mysterious figure was that of a protective spirit that spared her from serious – if not fatal – injury. Photographer Sharon Boo was kind enough to submit the original negative to confirm its validity and belives that 'she had an angel looking over her shoulder.'

'Could this be photographic evidence of a guardian angel?'

Bobbi's Ghoul in the Hot Tub

Bobbi Myers has always had a feeling that she and her family have a guardian spirit, and now she has the picture to prove it. This photograph was taken in November 1996 when Bobbi and her sisters holidayed in a mountain retreat. When the film was developed Bobbi was astonished to see that an uninvited misty figure had also joined them there. After discovering what she had captured on film Bobbi was happy to finally validate what she had always believed – that a friendly entity was part of her life.

'Bobbi was happy to finally validate what she had always felt – a friendly entity was part of her life...'

The obvious explanation for the presence of the mist would be the steam from the hot tub; however, there are no outside vents on the tub that could cause such an occurrence. Although a certain amount of steam can build up on the surface of the water, it generally doesn't settle so densely in one particular place, especially outside of the tub. Since the picture was developed three separate photo specialists have examined it and all were amazed at what they saw. They have ruled out a number of possibilities: it is not a flaw in the film or the developing process, and the negative has not been tampered with in any way. Whatever the explanation it certainly looks as though a ghostly presence is leaning over the tub, as if it were part of the group.

Spirit in the Mist

This photo is taken from a live webcam site where ghost enthusiasts can go to watch supernatural activity. The cameras usually refresh every 15 seconds and when you see something questionable, you simply right click and save the image to your hard drive. This particular picture was submitted to ghoststudy.com from Liz in Picayune, Mississippi, USA. She was thrilled to capture a possible ectoplasm surrounding a group of young women, but she says that the most extraordinary thing is the face that appears within the mist.

As with any ectoplasm photo we have to take into account other elements that may be responsible for the mist, such as moisture, or if the temperature was low then breath can be a contributing factor. However, we can see that the girls are dressed for summer which suggests that it is more likely to be something supernatural rather than cold breath on the lens.

'the most extraordinary thing is the face that appears within the mist...'

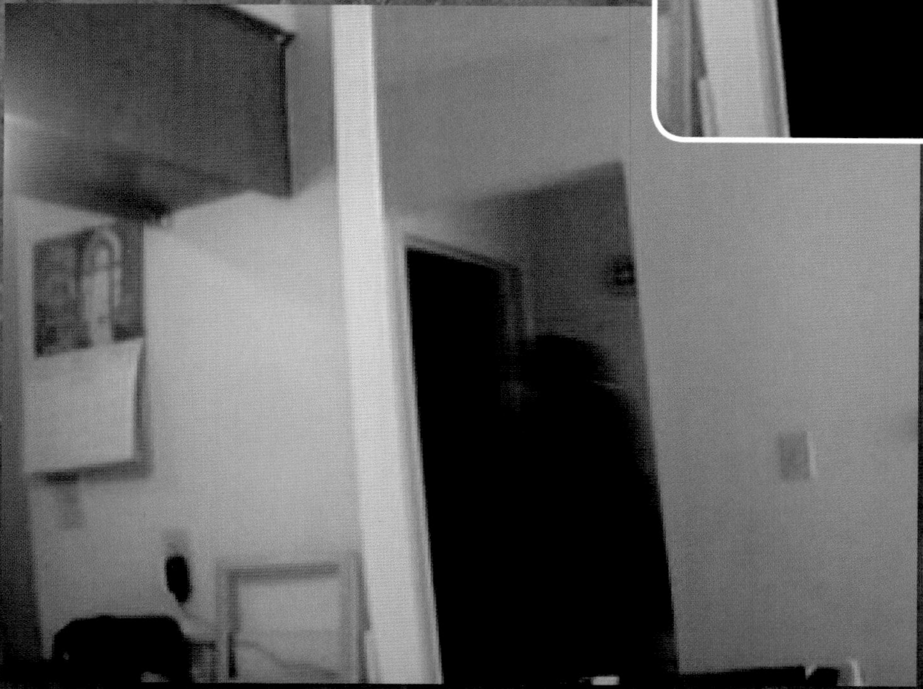

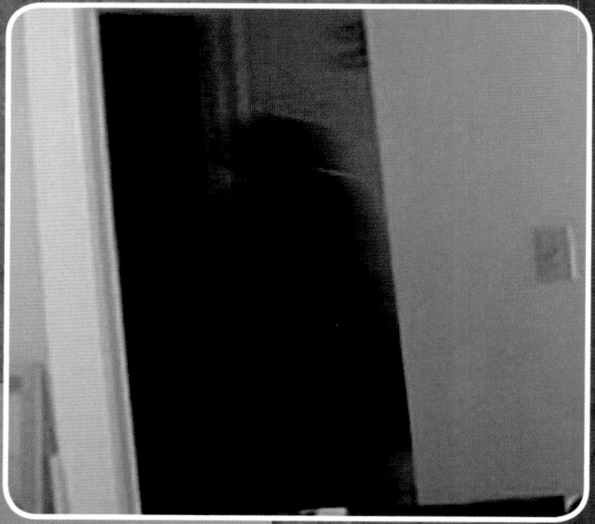

Fleeting Shadow Ghost

Megan was home alone and installing new software for her webcam. She had directed the camera away from her during the software installation and it was aimed towards the hallway but was still operating. The camera is programmed to take pictures every 5 seconds which are then placed on to a photo strip. Megan happened to glance at the strip and did a double take at a blob that had appeared in one of the captures. On closer inspection, she became convinced that this was a shadowy figure. Megan attempted to recreate the photo several times but she was unable to achieve similar results. Ghost research has found that home repair or remodelling often stirs up ghostly activity – was it a coincidence that an engineer had visited the day before to install new wiring in the attic?

If this was just a shadow, then why does it appear to be in motion when the rest of the frame is still? There can be no doubt that this picture may be of a ghost, however, we cannot completely rule out a living person in dark clothes either.

'home repair often stirs up ghostly activity...'

Veiled Woman in Mirror

This photo of Dan MacDonald was taken in 1983 when he was six years old. It was his first day back at school after suffering three months of viral pneumonia. During his illness he claims to have been visited one night by a veiled woman. He normally would have been afraid of a stranger's presence, but she had had a calming effect on him and watched over him until he drifted off to sleep. Amazingly, the very next day he was practically cured. Dan asked his mother about the veiled woman who had come to his room, but she dismissed it as a hallucination brought about by the virus.

It wasn't until 20 years later that Dan's mother stumbled across this photograph of her son taken on that first day back at school following his illness. In the framed picture in the background she noticed the reflection of a veiled woman watching over her son. Perhaps he hadn't been hallucinating after all! Dan is sure that this was the very same veiled woman that he saw in his room just a few nights prior. As for analysis, we know that the focal point of the flash is at the bottom left but that doesn't necessarily explain the woman's image above. However, Dan does feel that this ghostly portrait provides an answer to his mystery visitor during his childhood.

'Dan told his mother about the veiled woman who had come to his room...'

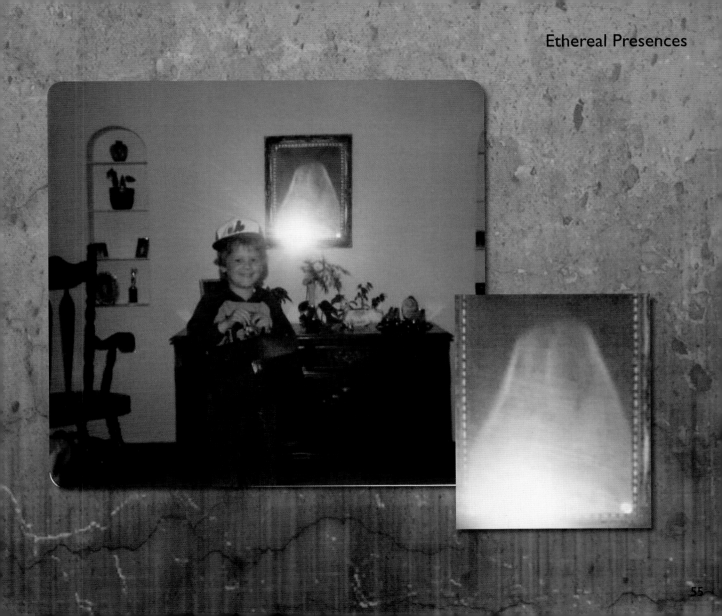

Welcome to the Asylum

This photo comes to us from Asylumcam.com. The creators of the site are a family who own a large three-story home in Sedalia, in the US state of Missouri, that they claim is haunted. They have set up webcams throughout the premises so that people from all over the world can log onto the site to watch the ghostly comings and goings, and the site posts many of the best images on their forums for all to see. This particular photo was submitted by Ophelia, who was watching the cameras when a sudden white flash popped up. She insists that the flash was a human figure and she believes it to be a spirit, or an angel.

'A sudden white flash popped up...'

We do have to take into consideration that this is a household with a family living in it and this could just be a motion blur of a living resident; however, in this particular image the figure is in the air and not on the stairs. So unless Ophelia captured a living person jumping off the stairs, we would have to consider the possibility that this could be a spirit.

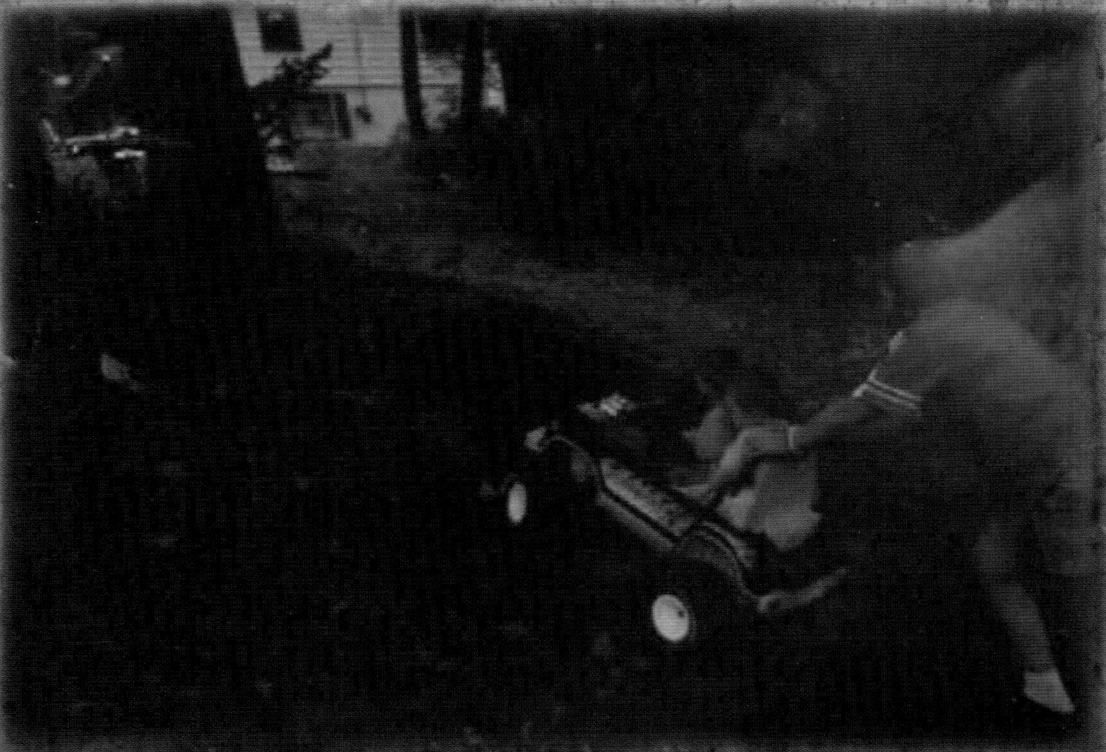

Healing Spirit

It's not often that we see a blue ghost in a photo. Kim took this photo of her friend with a 35mm camera at a family gathering. Her friend was playing with the children, despite suffering from a painful migraine. The friend reported that her headache disappeared soon after and the developed photo may show the reason why.

Kim's friend is pushing the children in their toy car, when the picture reveals a ghostly blue figure laying its hands on her head. Closer inspection shows that the figure is either wearing a robe or has wings. It appears that she is receiving a healing blessing from a supernatural being.

'the picture reveals a ghostly blue figure laying its hands on her head...'

Cameras are a wonderful tool in our efforts to capture the unseen at times, and once in a while, if we are really lucky, something extraordinary develops.

59

Wales' Most Haunted Castle?

The historic splendour of Craig-y-Nos castle attracts many visitors each year, and the ghosts seem to appreciate it too. The castle in the Brecon Beacons, south Wales has quite a reputation for paranormal activity, but it was all just rumour until a group of psychic investigators delivered the photographic proof that it was indeed haunted.

In 2004 an investigative team from the Jason Karl's Ghost Research Foundation (JKGRF) were investigating reports of supernatural sightings at the castle when psychic Paul Howse sensed an unusual presence on the staircase. The room was pitch black and the team were using infrared night vision in zero light conditions. It wasn't until they downloaded the pictures that they had taken that they realized what they had captured. The figure on the stairs even matches the eyewitness descriptions of ghostly encounters at the castle. Could it be that the psychic did actually sense a disembodied soul on the stairs and that we are seeing the proof?

"As I was going up the stair
I met a man who wasn't there
He wasn't there again today
I wish, I wish he'd stay away."

Hughes Mearns, 'Antigonish', 1899

'a group of psychic investigators delivered the photographic evidence that it was indeed haunted...'

HEAVENLY VISIONS

The images featured in this chapter have a spiritual significance of some form or other. Some of the pictures are quite bizarre, such as Sacred Sandwich $28,000 on pages 64–65, which tells the story of an online casino that paid big bucks for a half-eaten sandwich that bore the image of the Virgin Mary. Other pictures are strange but beautiful, such as Angel on the Water, pages 86–87, taken by a couple on their vacation. All the pictures are unique in their own way. Whether you are religious or agnostic, you will undoubtedly find them interesting.

Images with heavenly significance seem to be everywhere. A simple search on the web will render a mountain of them.

Generally, pictures that claim to offer evidence of an afterlife or to show heavenly beings are more carefully scrutinized. I make no claims that any of the photos featured in this chapter are authentic; however I do think that these are among the best that I have seen.

One particular photo sent to Ghoststudy.com appears to be of an image of Christ etched into the brickwork. Rose-Mary claimed that many similar images had appeared in her house over the years and all feature the same spiritual subject. You can view the photo on pages 66–67 and judge for yourself.

Sacred Sandwich $28,000

A grilled cheese sandwich bearing the image of the Virgin Mary was eventually sold on eBay for $28,000. The auction took place in 2004 and the winning bidder was an online casino, GoldenPalace.com who bought the partially eaten sandwich with the intention of using it to raise money for charity.

It was ten years earlier that Diane Duyser took a bite of her grilled cheese sandwich and was astonished to see a face looking back at her. She didn't finish the sandwich and decided to preserve its holy image by placing it in a plastic box with cotton balls. It sat around her house for a decade before she decided to share it with the world, and Diane even offered proof of its sacredness as the fact that it had survived all that time without a trace of mould growing on it.

This is a classic case of pareidolia, an optical illusion where we see something we want to see or which has been suggested to us, rather than what is actually there. Either that or the Virgin Mary really has chosen to reveal herself in a toasted cheese sandwich!

'she was astonished to see a face looking back at her...'

Rose-Mary's Haunted House

Rose-Mary was used to carvings and stains in the form of words and religious symbols appearing on the walls of her haunted Welsh farmhouse. She even received the occasional image of a monk or the face of a girl appearing out of nowhere. But she was particularly shocked to discover an image above the fireplace which resembled the tortured, haunted face of a crucified Christ. A few days after the face emerged, the word IUDAEUS (Latin for Jew, or of Judea) was found above the image, followed by the word CHRISTUS (Latin for Christ) below the face.

Rose-Mary and her family have no explanation for the mysterious images and scripture which adorn their home, but as long as they continue to be harmless, then she and her family will continue to feel privileged to be favoured this way.

'It resembled the tortured, haunted face of a crucified Christ...'

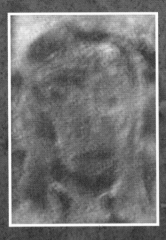

Other images that have appeared

Spirit in the Sky

This picture of a spiritual manifestation was taken in Guam and it was meant to be a simple scenic shot of the beach and sky. It was only after the film was developed that the figure in the clouds was noticed.

Pictures similar to this are quite common, but one of such clarity is rare. Look closely at the figure – it has the proportions of a human being and appears to be wearing a hooded robe. You may even be inclined to think that it is a spiritual vision. But at the same time we can't completely rule out explanations such as a spot on the lens or even some type of airborne particle which is close to the lens.

'it appears to be wearing a hooded robe...'

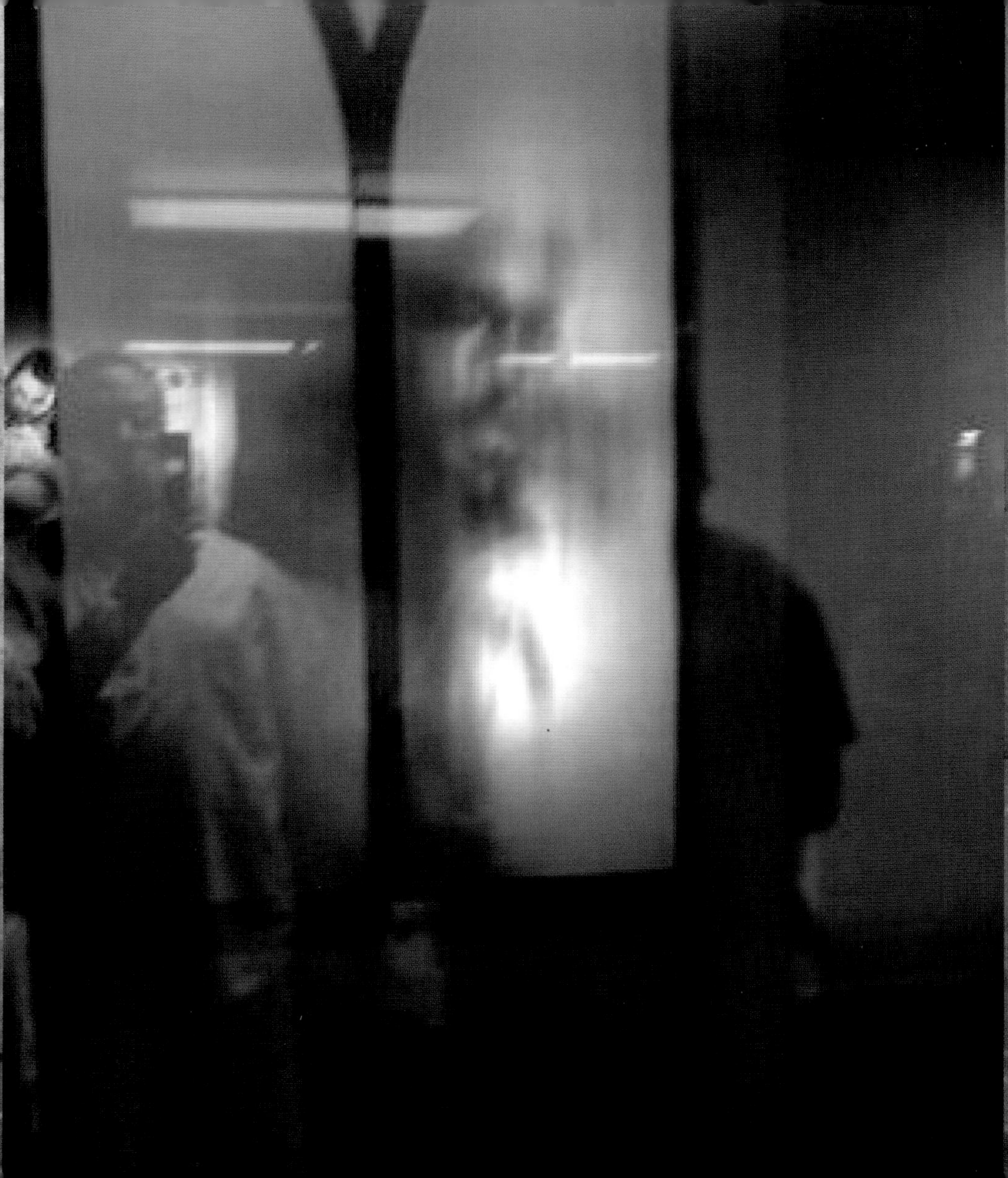

Jesus the Healer

The Bible teaches that Jesus was a healer – wherever he went people would bring their sick to him to be healed. How appropriate then that an image of Jesus should appear in a hospital medical complex in Orlando, Florida, USA, in a hallway that overlooked the prayer garden. After one person noticed the spiritual vision, a crowd of people soon gathered round, watching in awe and taking lots of photographs.

One witness implied that the 'vision' was the result of leaves pressing up against the acrylic panels, creating the dark shadows that formed the 'face'. It was a windy and rainy day so this could explain why the image would reportedly change shape at times. After a few hours the vision of Christ had completely vanished. The image has not been seen since, but that's not to say that it won't re-emerge in the future. Whatever the explanation, it was at least, for some, a sign that a higher being was watching over their loved ones in their greatest hour of need.

'a sign that a higher being was watching over their loved ones...'

Virgin Mary's Mirror Image

The human image in the window of this office building in Clearwater, Florida, USA is thought to be an apparition of the Virgin Mary. She was first noticed in December 1996 as she appeared in rainbow hues on nine large panes of bronze coloured glass. Within the first 30 days of the appearance, it is estimated that over half a million people flocked to see the phenomenal apparition.

Unfortunately this extraordinary representation of the Virgin Mary was not to last and a young man was arrested in 2004 for destroying the three upper glass panels, which wiped out her draped robe-covered head. The crowds still come to be marvel at what remains of this remarkable spiritual manifestation and the smashed glass fragments from the vandalism incident have even come up for sale on eBay. The building – Our Lady of Clearwater – is now owned by Shepherds of Christ Ministries who welcome all visitors.

'Unfortunately this extraordinary representation of the Virgin Mary was not to last ...'

Heaven's Answer

To many this may just look like an old, worn photograph, but to the original owner it was a precious possession that she carried around with her at all times as a source of inspiration and to remind her to never give up hope even in the most difficult of circumstances. Many years previously, back in 1967, she had been going through a particularly traumatic period in her life and had started to doubt her faith. Unable to take anymore, she ran outside and screamed to the heavens, asking her God why she had been burdened so. As soon as she had exhausted her rage, the sky darkened and it began to thunder and a vision of Jesus Christ appeared in the sky. The woman took this as a sign that her questions had been answered, and ran to retrieve her camera from the house so that she could capture on film this spectacular message of hope from the heavens.

Some say that this is no more than an illusion created by atmospheric conditions at the time but, others believe that this really was God's answer to the woman's plea for help. Whichever view you take, this picture was enough to restore at least one person's faith and hope.

'She took this as a sign that her questions had been answered...'

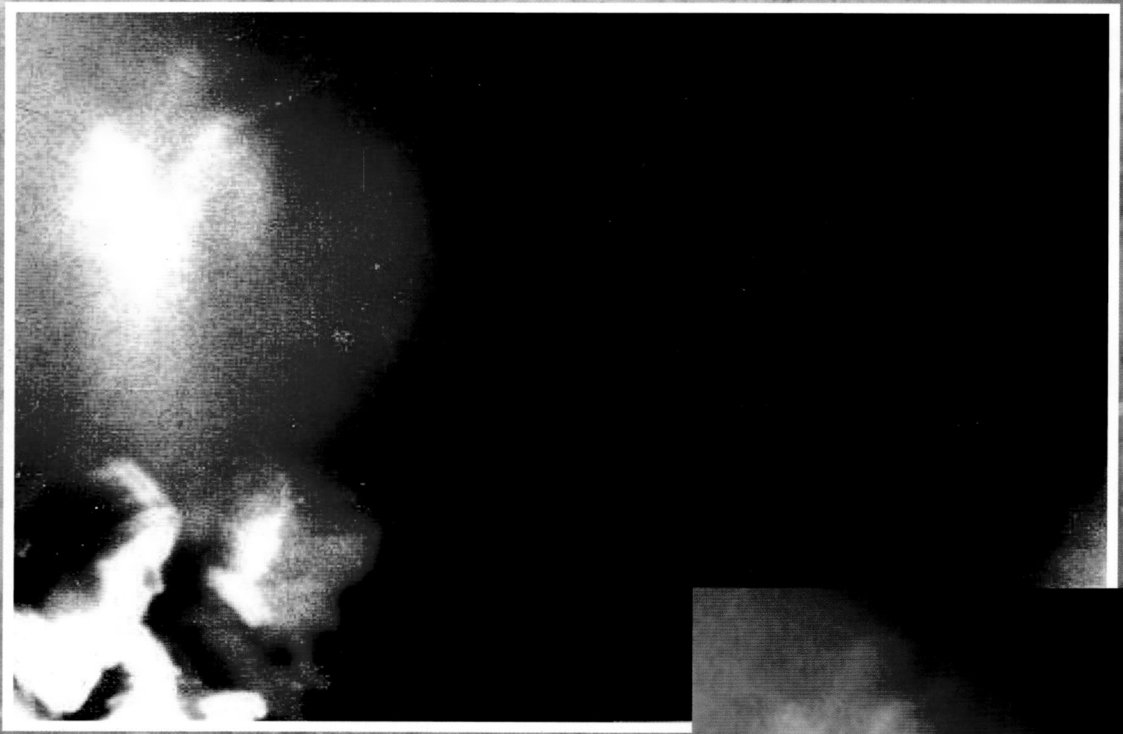

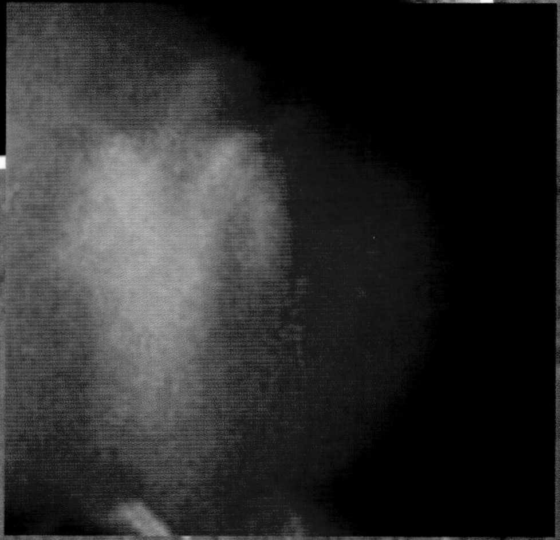

Protector of the Camp

A young group from Skycrest Christian School in Clearwater, Florida, USA were at their youth camp when a biker gang rode into the camp and began to harass and terrorize them. Then, without explanation, the biker gang disappeared as quickly as they had arrived. It appeared that something, or someone had frightened them off. This picture was taken shortly after the incident and appears to provide an answer to the question, why did the bikers leave in such a hurry?

The group and their leaders believe that this photo clearly displays a guardian angel protecting them from their unwelcome visitors. Dozens of people witnessed the event and hundreds within the church viewed the photo after the incident, which certified the strength in faith for many. Whether it was an anomaly created by the campfire or whether it really is an image of their heavenly protector, the campers were obviously protected by some unseen force that day.

'Something, or someone had frightened them off...'

Fiery Crucifix

This photograph was sent to me by Brett Simonsen, a member of the congregation of St John's Lutheran Church in Norfolk, Nebraska, USA. As Brett will tell you, there is only one cross in the grounds of the church and it's located in the bell tower. And yet, the picture quite plainly shows a second cross – a crucifix. Incredibly this second cross was a fleeting vision that lasted less than a few seconds.

On the night of August 18, 2001, church members gathered for a celebration. Photographer Steve Montgomery recorded the event with his 35mm camera, setting the exposure to 4 seconds to capture the wonder of the fireworks display. When the film was developed one photograph in particular caught the eye. The fireworks had formed into a crucifix, and although the image of Christ vanished almost at once, if you look carefully at the picture you can clearly see Jesus hanging from the cross.

'you can clearly see Jesus hanging from the cross...'

The good people of St John's church feel they have something truly special in this photograph and that this is indeed a sign of their faith.

Hiker's Discovery

A missing branch in a tree is nothing unusual, however if you look carefully you can see that it gives the distinct likeness of what many people describe to be the Virgin Mary and baby Jesus. The tree was discovered by three hikers who were new to the area. They couldn't help but notice the prominent figures displayed there. At first they thought it was just a trick of the light, but after they got up close to the tree they could see that it was an optical illusion caused by the missing branch. The scene miraculously displays the perfect image of Mary and the Christ child, and you can even see a halo above each of the figures.

The images within the tree are just as striking up-close and many locals believe that they have been blessed by a miracle. The figures are so lifelike, they even have facial features and hairlines. It's an extraordinary find.

'The scene miraculously displays the perfect image of Mary and the Christ child...'

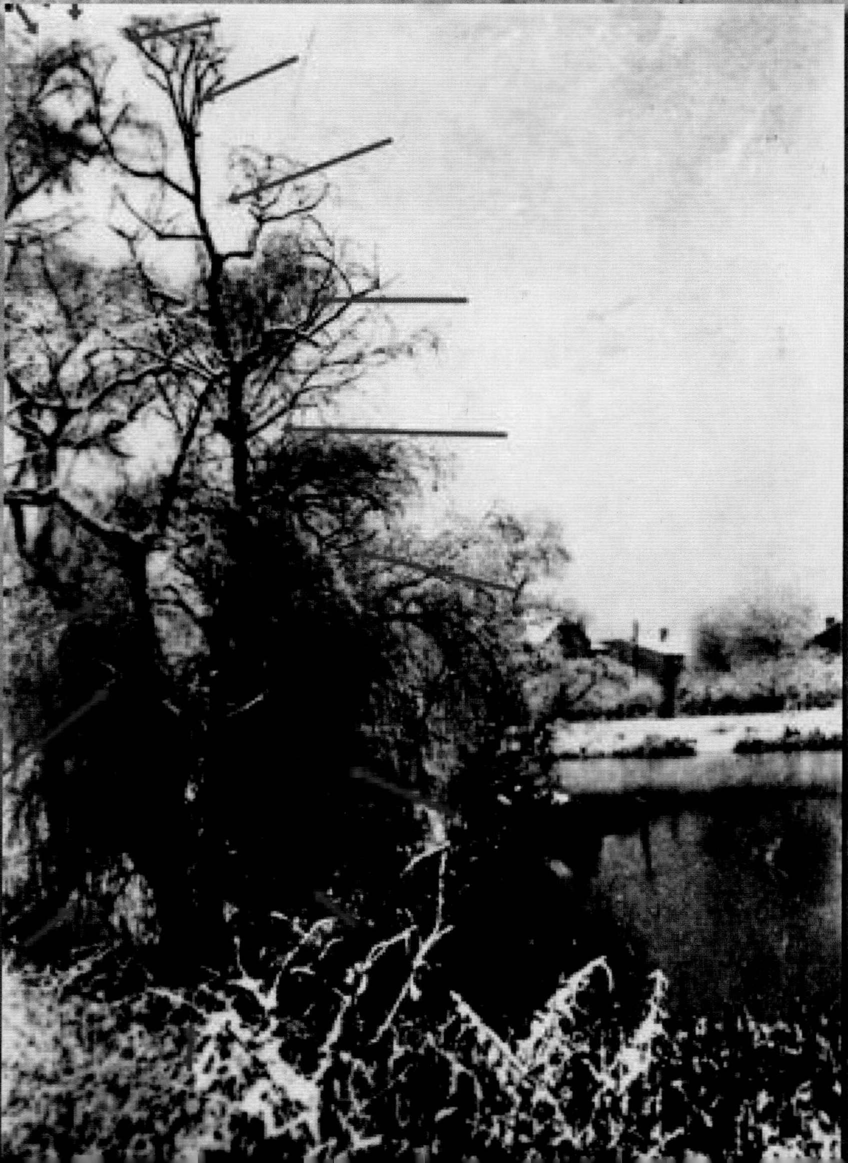

Image of Jesus in Tree

In 1936 a young family made the big decision to move to the USA from their hometown in Brazil. After staying with a relative for two years, they began looking for their own place and in March 1938 they took this picture of a property that they were hoping to buy. Once they saw the developed photo, they knew that their decision to buy the house was the right one as the picture contained a sign from heaven – an image of Christ. They kept the picture safe in their family Bible for many years and they prospered from their newly purchased land, feeling blessed for the heavenly assistance they had in making their decision to move there.

This picture has been studied meticulously over the last few years and the majority conclude that the image of Jesus is actually part of a tree. Most people can see Jesus wearing a crown of thorns and looking up to the heaven.

'Most people can see Jesus wearing a crown of thorns and looking up to heaven...'

Figure of Light in Cathedral

This photo was taken in a cathedral in the UK, and has been circulating the web for many years although its origin is unknown. The photograph appears to be aged and stained and it's likely that it was displayed in the owner's home for many years. Regardless of age, it seems to have a spiritual significance for many who view it. There is a figure standing above a podium and behind a safety railing. There's no evidence of a bright light source in front of the figure, yet it has a bright, white glow.

Some may suspect that photo manipulation has been used to create the image and this should always be a consideration when we have little information about the picture. However, it's also a possibility that this is evidence of a spirit, especially when we consider the location in which the picture was taken.

'There's no evidence of a bright light source in front of the figure, yet it has a bright, white glow...'

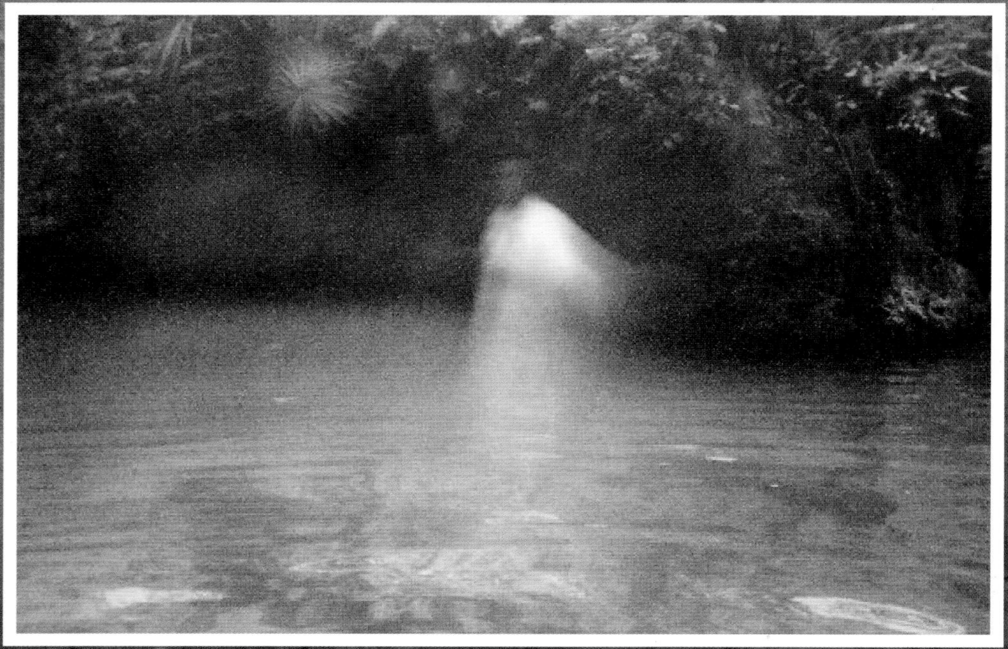

Angel on the Water

This amazing photograph was captured by Ron and Linda Martinez on their holiday in Cancun, Mexico using a 35mm disposable underwater camera. They only discovered the astonishing image when they returned home and had the pictures developed. The 'angel' even appears on the negative.

The photo has yet to be explained, despite being analyzed by many professionals including photographers, graphics experts, imaging specialists, psychics, paranormal societies and even Photoshop experts. It may be an angel, a spirit, or a ghost. It may even be a freak exposure or a ray of light caught through a drop of water on the lens; however many believe that this stunning image is photographic evidence of an angel walking on water.

'The photo has yet to be explained, despite being analyzed by many professionals...'

Vision in the Clouds

We all like to do a little cloud spotting and to marvel at the shapes revealed by them, but Beatrice Mielke couldn't believe her eyes when she saw this vision emerge from the skies across O'Shaughnessy Dam near Columbus, Ohio, USA. It was approaching sunset on a Sunday in 1972 when the image of Jesus appeared in the clouds, surrounded by light radiating in all directions. For Beatrice, a committed Christian, it was an answer to her fervent prayers.

This is an enduring image: whether it is the result of the atmospheric conditions on the day, or a tantalizing glimpse of heaven, there is no doubt that it is a classic feel-good photo moment. Yes, cloud shapes may be commonplace, but this one demands our attention.

'The image of Jesus appeared in the clouds, surrounded by light radiating in all directions...'

INTO THE PHYSICAL REALM

It is a widely accepted belief that various entity types can attach themselves to inanimate objects. So not only can you have ghosts living in your house, you can also find them attached to your belongings and that is the basis for the images in this chapter.

One of the first things ghost investigators consider during a paranormal investigation is the possibility of a haunted object having been brought into the home from an antique store, a garage sale, or an online auction site. Second-hand jewellery is particularly susceptible to haunting, and can carry either negative energy or a ghost/entity attachment. What's the

difference? If you purchase a second-hand necklace and, when you wear it, you feel depressed, anxious or upset, it is likely that it has a negative energy associated with it – bury it in salt for several days to dispel the energy. A ghost/entity attachment is not so easy to resolve: the second-hand item has 'carried' a haunting into your home, and you may need to get rid of it. Do not destroy the object or you may invite retaliation from the ghost; do not pass it on to someone else unless you make it very clear what they are taking on; do bury it in a box out of harm's way far from your home.

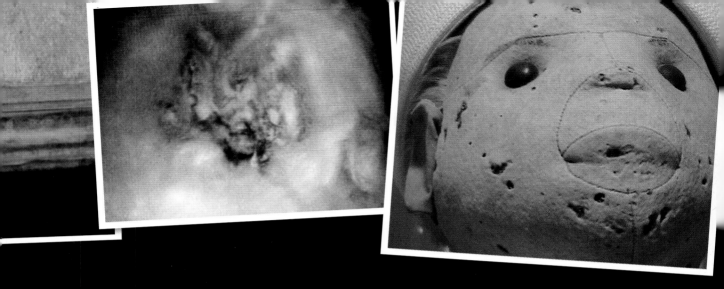

Ghost/entity attachments will not necessarily cause a problem. Take for example Vincent the Walking Clown on pages 94–95; he may be haunted but he is not much trouble – he may move around from time to time, voices may be overheard, but otherwise he is a friendly haunting. The same cannot be said of the two haunted jars (Ghost in a Jar, pages 98–99, and Vampire in a Jar, pages 100–101) which contain, it is claimed, terrorizing and murderous entities. How is the entity not able to pass through the glass to free itself? Three possible explanations have been offered, and in this case:

1. Certain types of entities cannot pass through solid objects.
2. A containment spell was either written on the jar or spoken verbally.
3. There was no such entity in the container to begin with.

The containment spell seems to apply for the Ghost in a Jar, and it could also apply to the Vampire in a Jar. And as for the third option, it would be a brave person who opens either of these containers to find this out.

Ghost Squashed in a Book

A distributor of second-hand books claimed to have found a ghost squashed inside an old textbook. He suspected its remains may have been trapped inside for decades and slime – possibly ectoplasm – had stained the book's pages.

The book distributor was offering this unique item for auction on eBay, and the good-natured bidding that ensued shows that even ghost hunters have a sense of humour.

'He suspected its remains may have been trapped inside for decades...'

Vincent the Walking Clown

When Ernest, a doll sculptor, bought Vincent he thought it would be the perfect model for his own work. But when he brought the clown home weird things began happening. He'd hear little children whispering and giggling, and the sound of footsteps. He would leave the doll in one place, and when he returned to the room it would have moved to another spot. Was it possible that the doll was haunted by a previous child owner? Uncomfortable keeping it in his house, he decided to put it up for auction on eBay.

The doll was advertised as being in excellent condition and the only visible signs of wear-and-tear were on the soles of its shoes, which were clearly worn, faded and patched, undoubtedly a result of its wanderlust. Arousing a great deal of interest, Vincent sold in November 2002 for $430.

'to this day Vincent still continues to move around her house...'

The doll's new owner, Renée, reports that to this day Vincent continues to move around her house – not everyday, just when the mood seems to take him.

Robert the Haunted Doll

If you're ever in Key West, Florida, be sure to visit East Martello Museum where you will find Robert the haunted doll, which is easily the museum's most popular exhibit.

In 1904 the Otto family nanny created a doll to resemble the boy that she looked after – Robert Eugene. The doll measured 3ft (1m) tall and was stuffed with straw – even the doll's hair is believed to have been taken from Robert Eugene himself. When the boy was presented with the doll he immediately became fixated by it, even sacrificing his own name (Robert) to it and thereafter insisting on being called by his middle name, Eugene (Gene), instead. Soon after he had been given his gift, strange occurrences began to happen in the home. Schoolchildren would notice the doll's eyes following them from the window and it wasn't long before people started to avoid the Otto home altogether. Finally Gene's mother decided to place the toy away in the attic, where it was soon forgotten. After the death of Gene's parents, Gene and Robert were reunited once more, but it was short-lived as Gene's wife placed the doll back in the attic where it stayed until Gene's death.

The doll is now over 100 years old and is displayed in the museum where many mishaps are blamed on him. Robert receives fan mail each week which are posted on the museum walls. So when visiting Robert, be kind enough to ask for permission for any photos you may take of him before he starts misbehaving for you too.

'Schoolchildren would notice the doll's eyes following them as they passed the window...'

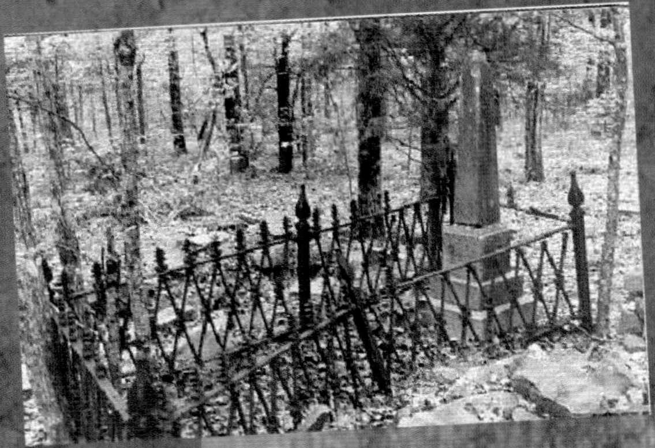

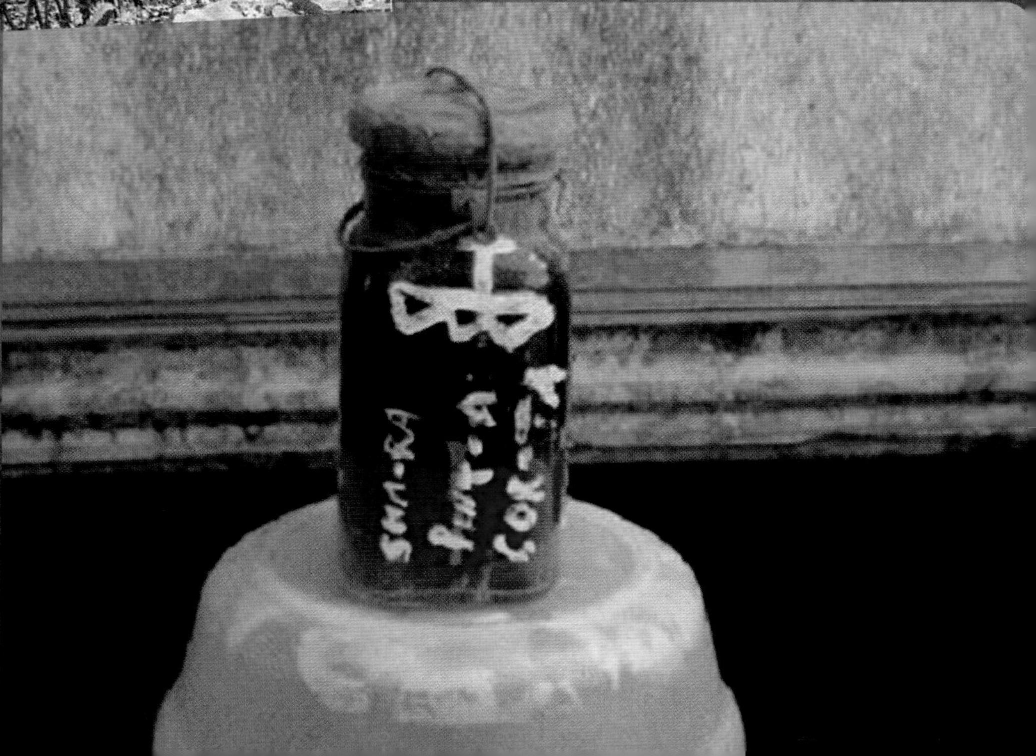

Famous Ghost in a Jar

On March 26, 2003 the ghost in a jar was put up for auction on eBay. Teajay, the owner of the unusual lot, claimed that he had in his possession a real ghost contained within a sealed jar. The bidding started at $99 and quickly grew.

Some 20 years earlier Teajay had been out with his metal detector, investigating the grounds of an abandoned cemetery. Among the foundations of an old building he found a wooden box with metal hinges and a clasp. Within the decaying box lay two jars adorned with mysterious writing and symbols, along with an old journal. Startled by his find, Teajay accidentally dropped one of the jars and from the broken shards of glass emerged a dark misty figure. Petrified, he fled the cemetery with the remaining jar and journal. Once he reached the safety of home, he opened the fragile book and claims that what he read within the pages of the old journal before they crumbled away was truly frightening. That night the black mist from the jar returned to haunt him and attacked him in his bed, but fortunately he managed to escape after a struggle.

'what he read within the pages of the old journal before they crumbled away was truly frightening...'

Over the years Teajay endured two more encounters with the black mist – curiously it was usually when the jar was nearby. No longer wanting to be tormented by such an evil presence, he was advised to pass the jar on to someone else so that the black mist would follow, and he decided to auction it. The successful bidder would receive the sealed jar, additional photographs and Teajay's account of what he could recall from his reading of the journal. After fervent bidding, the final offer was an astonishing $50,992. The auction excited great interest, and was viewed an incredible 830,000 times. There has been no word from the seller or the buyer since the auction, so the jar, its contents, and those involved remain a mystery.

2222222

2222232

232322222222

Vampire in a Jar

In August 2001 Hairul Hambali, a bomoh (spiritual healer) from the Sabak Bernam district in Selangor, Malaya, claimed he had captured a vampire in a jar. Word soon spread of the imprisoned creature and a television crew were allowed to record Hambali as he placed a spell on the jar to safely contain its contents.

Malaysian folklore is rich with stories of demon-vampires. Hambali's captive was a langsuir, a particularly nasty entity that can possess, terrorize and even kill its victims. It is said that this type of vampire is able to change form to suit its surroundings, so when Hambali found the langsuir hiding near a cotton tree, it is not surprising that it resembled a wad of cotton. The Malaysian newspaper, *The Straits Times* reported that it was the size of two tennis balls with a little face.

The media coverage of Hambali's story provoked huge public interest and people from all over the country flocked to see the vampire in a jar. Hambali, overcome by the attention, is said to have thrown the jar into the sea to rid himself of it. Let us hope that the caged murderer has disappeared forevermore.

'it was the size of two tennis balls with a little face...'

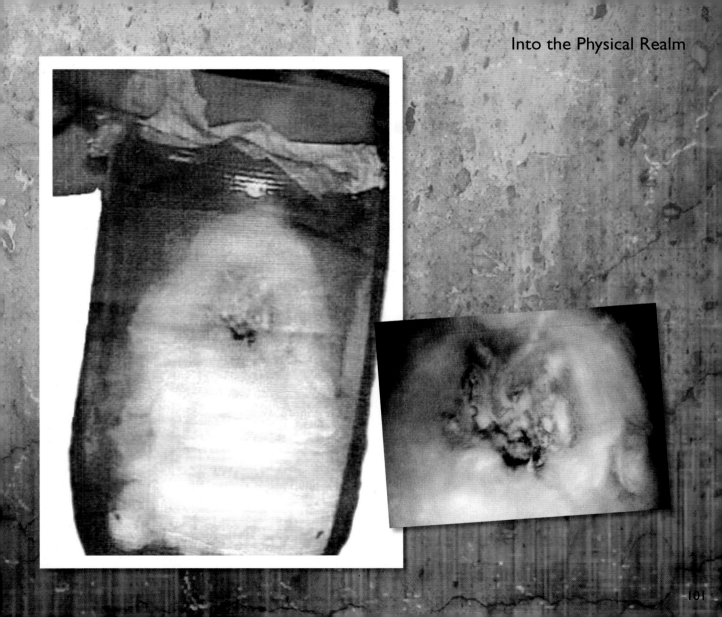

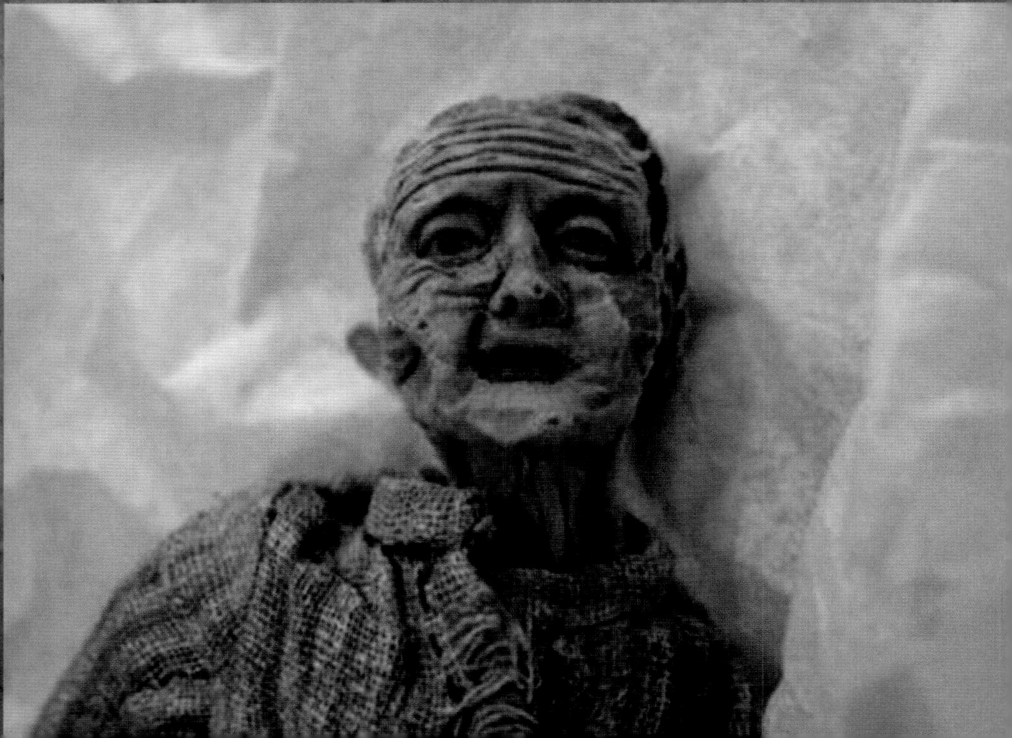

The Doll that Grew Old

Paranormal investigators often hear of possessions that disappear, change shape or even materialize out of thin air, but a doll that can age right in front of your very eyes is exceptional.

The family who originally bought the doll purchased it in very good condition and they say it was a typical, youthful looking toy. As time went on, they noticed that the doll underwent a distinct aging process. They decided to store it in the attic, and when they stumbled upon it 11 years later, they were shocked by how much it had aged – it looked decrepit, withered and wrinkled like an old man. Horrified by its condition, the frightened family gave it away to an interested couple they knew. It wasn't long however, before it was sold on eBay for a considerable amount of money. This is the picture that was taken just before the doll was given away by the family. We can only wonder what condition it may be in now.

'it looked decrepit, withered and wrinkled like an old man...'

GHOSTS IN THE HOUSE

It seems that most ghost pictures are taken by happenstance. A picture is snapped and lo and behold, strange figures show up in the photo! Interestingly enough, most people don't even notice the ghost images in their photos until they begin to look for them. So, if you fancy the life of a ghost hunter, start by checking through your photo albums.

If you happen to have a ghost in your house, you are not alone. Do your keys regularly disappear only to be discovered somewhere other than where you left them? Maybe you aren't losing

your mind after all. Keep an eye out for the tell-tale signs of a haunting; some of these may seem insignificant and can easily be overlooked, but if more than a few of these ring a bell with you, you may have an uninvited guest in your home.

Signs of a haunting
1. Feeling of being watched.
2. Voices out of nowhere.
3. The sound of footsteps.
4. Household objects mysteriously disappearing only to be found elsewhere.
5. The phone ringing but no one is there when it

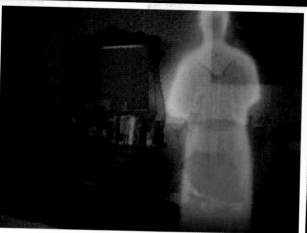

is answered.

6. Strange odours that have no source.

7. Lights or appliances being turned on or off.

8. Animals acting strangely.

9. Books or other objects being thrown off shelves.

10. Cold spots.

11. Feeling of being touched.

12. Appearance of a transparent being.

13. Feeling of sadness.

14. Strange shadows.

15. Cabinets opening and closing.

How does one get rid of a ghost in their house? It depends on the haunting, the type of ghost or entity, and why it's there. Those who believe they may be haunted would be advised to contact a local group of ghost hunters or investigators to see what they can recommend.

The photos offered in this chapter are fascinating but be warned, you may end up sleeping with the lights on afterwards.

Uninvited Guest at Lodge

This extraordinary photograph of what appears to be a shadow ghost at a curtained window was taken in August 2004 at the Comstock Lodge in Virginia City, Nevada, USA by hotel guest Raul Juarez. There was no one else in his room when Raul took this photograph and he cannot find an explanation for the photographic anomaly. There is nothing in the room that could have cast such a shadow as this and, even more puzzling, there is no reflection of the shadowy figure in the mirror.

In the lightened photograph below you can see that the image resembles the shape of a man and you can detect a hat – a stereotypical trait of shadow beings. Ghost investigators state that Virginia City is notorious for being one of the most common places to experience the supernatural. Considering the photograph's integrity, location and detail, we can only assume that Raul was not alone in his room, as he had originally thought.

'We can only assume that Raul was not alone in the room, as he had originally thought...'

Shadow Ghost Grabs Child

Adam was browsing through his latest batch of developed family photographs when he came upon this terrifying image of what appears to be a shadow ghost grabbing hold of his young nephew. Understandably Adam feared for the little boy.

There have been several accounts of people being menaced and chased by shadow beings, but rarely attacked. It is incredible, therefore, to have an extraordinarily defined photograph of such an event. Closer inspection of this incredible photograph reveals that there may be even more to the story. Look to the left of the picture, at the boy's arm and shoulder. Can you see a white hand? And, just above the hand, is that a glimpse of a white face? Is there an attempt underway to rescue the boy from his shadow-being abductor? Could this be a case of good vs. evil? Happily on this occasion the shadow being was thwarted and we can report that the boy is safe and well.

'Could this be a case of good vs. evil?...'

Ghosts Caught on Film 2

Girl in the Door

This picture was taken after setting up a QuickCam on a new family computer. The owner of the picture claims that he was testing the camera by taking a few photographs, but he did not notice the image of the girl until two weeks later when he was going through the picture files. It looks as though a child is walking directly through the solid door.

Webcams like the QuickCam are becoming quite useful in the ghost hunting community. Ghost hunters set them up in a haunted location in the hope of catching an elusive ghost on film. This footage can also be shared with ghost enthusiasts online. But cam operators have to be careful not to make the mistake of identifying motion blur – caused when someone runs or walks quickly past the camera – as the presence of a ghost.

However this image does not exhibit the classic characteristics of motion blur (see page 154). Could the fact that a friend of the family passed away the night that this photo was taken provide an answer to why an apparition of a young girl should appear from nowhere?

'It looks as though a child is walking directly through the solid door...'

The Green Family Ghost

This old photograph of the Green family was being scanned by Josh for his online family tree, when he noticed something very unusual about it. The scanned image revealed that a white-hooded woman watching from the screen door was also posing for the camera that day.

Some might dismiss the ghostly figure as a classic example of double exposure, and yet if this were the case it is unlikely that the apparition would be so perfectly contained within the window frame. The lack of detail in the figure's face suggests that this is indeed a spectral apparition rather than a living person. Of course, we cannot completely rule out glare or reflection as the cause of the anomaly, but isn't it just possible that a deceased family member decided to show up for the photo call?

'a white-hooded woman watching from the screen door was also posing for the camera that day...'

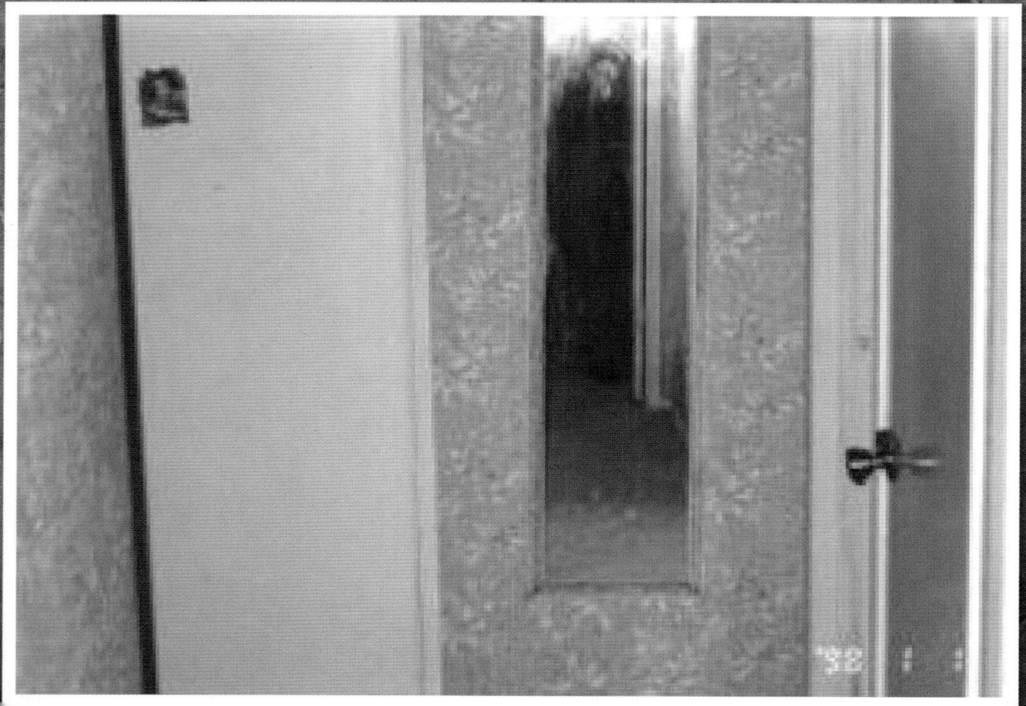

Haunted Mirror in the Hall

This picture first emerged at a ghost conference in Virginia City, Nevada, USA in 2002. Tony claimed that he had a haunted house that was especially active, and not only that, he also had the photographic evidence to prove it. Tony told onlookers that he had taken the picture of his hallway mirror whilst attempting to gather visual evidence of his hauntings. He was adamant that he was standing alone in the hallway.

The photo certainly seems to back up Tony's allegations that he had been haunted, however a reflection in the mirror – especially when cameras are involved – could also be a valid explanation for this figure. Although it could quite possibly be a dark entity of sorts, we still can't completely rule out a distorted reflection of Tony.

'He was adamant that he was standing alone in the hallway...'

Lady of the Mansion

In 2005 this picture was taken at the Bard Mansion on the Port Hueneme Naval Base in Ventura County, California, USA with an Olympus Stylus 4.0 megapixel camera. Thomas R. Bard was a California Senator from 1900–1905 and it is claimed that this is the apparition of Bard's wife. The second picture is of a close up of the apparition, which has been lightened.

Not everyone would agree that this is an authentic ghost photo and a true ghost hunter should never accept an image on face value. Do your own research and consider the integrity of the photographer and their transcript of the event. And finally gain an understanding of photography and how photo imaging programs work – the more you know, the better qualified you are to make a decision.

'it is claimed that this is the apparition of the Bard's wife...'

Ghosts on Fire

When Kerry heard that a friend's family home had been involved in a fire, she was just relieved to hear that they were all safe as they had been out watching a softball game at the time. Later when she saw the photos of the incident taken by the local fire department she couldn't believe her eyes. Were spirits trying to escape the flames?

In the burning smoke escaping from the top floor window some see a face of an old man with large staring eyeballs and a wide-open, maybe screaming, mouth. Others see three screaming heads with a tortured and twisted look on their faces. Looking back, the family recalls that there had been strange happenings in their home, and the toddler would often try to communicate with people who weren't there, or stretch out her arms to be picked up by an invisible being. So maybe the ghostly residents of the house were not as lucky as the living ones that day.

'three heads, with a tortured and twisted look on their faces...'

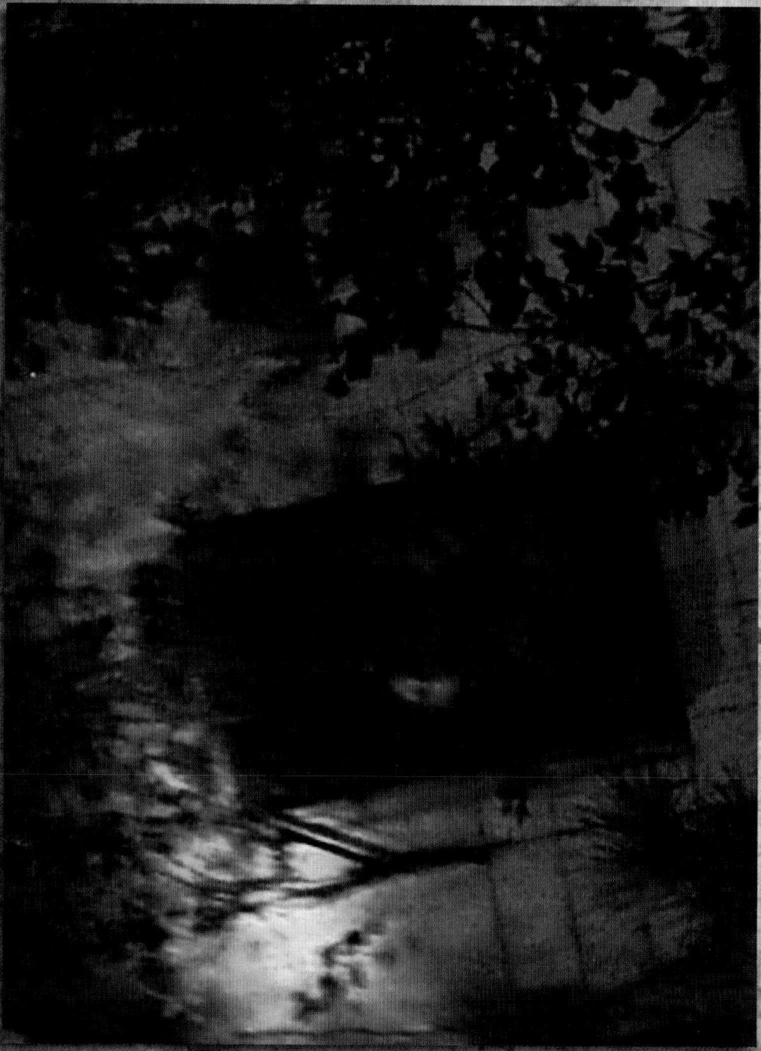

A Cry for Help

This old abandoned house in Lakeland, Florida, USA was the location of a terrible and tragic suicide where a young girl hanged herself many years before. The ghost hunting team that took the picture believes this to be photographic evidence of her lingering tormented soul.

This has all the signs of being a 'soft ghost' – rather than being an optical illusion there is the possibility that it is something paranormal, although it is impossible to say for sure. The ghost hunters' van was parked parallel to the window, so we can establish that its headlights were not directly facing the house and therefore we can discount glare or reflection as a cause of the ghostly image. The team took a few pictures before they fled the area. Did they feel an uncomfortable presence when they parked alongside the house that night, or did the image of the ghostly noose to the right of the picture frighten them away?

'The ghost hunting team...believes this to be photographic evidence of her lingering tormented soul...'

Phantom at the Window

This photo started circulating the web several years ago and has gathered a lot of attention ever since. It shows a rather evil-looking uninvited guest as a family prepares for their three-year-old's birthday party. Family friend Debbie submitted this photograph when she realized that the figure in the window was actually inside the house between the curtains and the window. She was quite alarmed by what she had captured on film, especially as there was no one in the house at the time.

Even if there was someone in the house, surely they wouldn't have looked like this! Although it could be a reflection or that something menacing had been placed in the window of the house, this picture was enough to unsettle not only the family but the thousands who have viewed it since.

'It shows a rather evil-looking uninvited guest...'

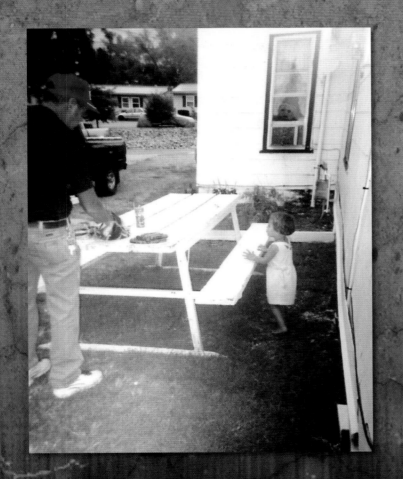

And Ghost Makes Three

Sean couldn't believe it when Carol, his girlfriend, showed him this bizarre picture of her aunt and uncle. The photo dates back to September 1980 and it resurfaced after it was found in a sealed envelope in her grandmother's possessions. Carol contacted her aunt and uncle who were oblivious that they had posed for a photograph beside a ghost.

There are several possible explanations for this ghostly effect. It may have been cigarette smoke in front of the lens although this is unlikely because of the amount of detail in the face, shirt, torso, and upper arm. It may also be glare or shadow; an optical illusion; or even photo manipulation. But then again it could truly be a ghost.

'they were oblivious that they had posed for a photograph beside a ghost...'

Night-vision Apparition

Dominic took this picture with a Sony DCR-TRV17 camera with the night vision setting on. This particular camcorder is a favourite among ghost hunters because it was one of the first to have night vision, which allows you to film and take pictures in the dark. Dominic had just recieved the camera and was experimenting with this setting by taking still shots around her house when this glowing image appeared in her bedroom. She claims to have seen it through the LCD screen twice and took a picture the second time that it appeared.

'this glowing image appeared in her bedroom...'

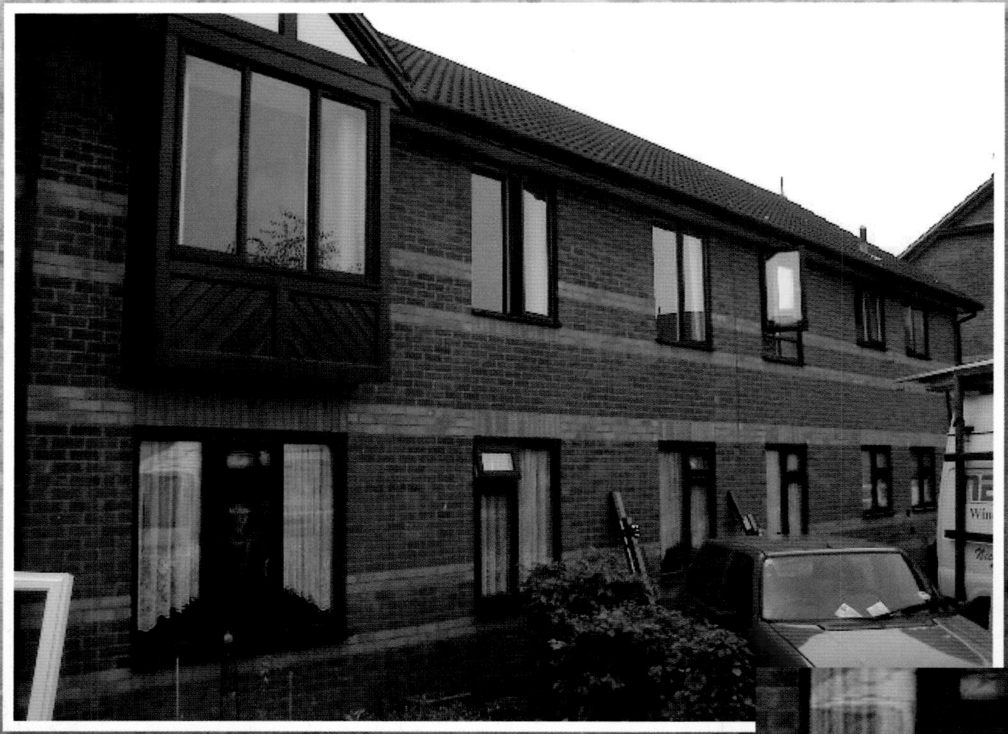

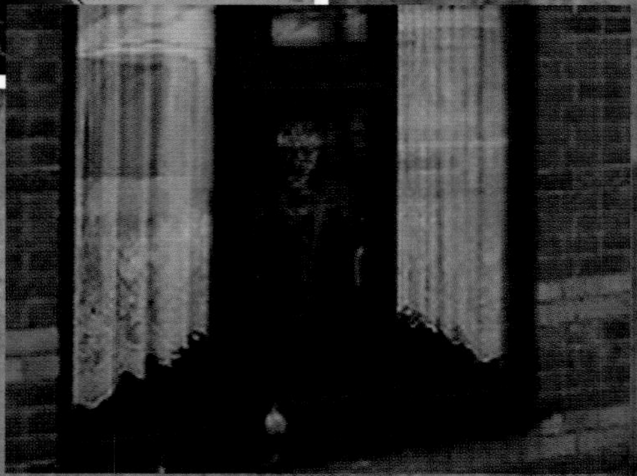

Ghost at the Window

Ashley works for a glazing company and took this picture of a housing-complex for elderly people after her company installed new glass windows there. A strange and menacing figure appeared in the window of the ground floor flat and yet the property was vacant at the time.

Who or what might this be? Given that the windows are newly installed and therefore clean and clear, it is unlikely that this effect has been caused by smudging or glare on the glass. Perhaps a tenant who has passed away is unwilling to move on and is making his presence known from beyond the grave? It certainly invites debate.

'the strange and menacing figure appeared in the window of the ground floor flat...'

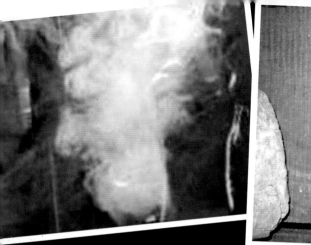

TRICK OF THE LIGHT?

When looking at the ghostly images in the photographs featured in this chapter I cannot rule out that there may be a logical explanation for their occurrence: it is more than likely that they are optical illusions, created by a trick of the light. For example, the Screaming Ghost on page 138–139 – in spite of its amazingly realistic look, it is most likely to have arisen from natural abnormalities in the wood.

Clouds are a perfect example of how we can allow our mind to trick us into seeing shapes and images

of smoke and dust particles can have the same effect, producing images that trick us into reaching a supernatural explanation. Leafy trees and gnarled branches can give us fleeting images of an unusual nature, but return next week when the tree has grown, and the anomaly is likely to have disappeared. Instances of all of these will be seen in this chapter.

The trick of the light is sometimes obvious to some, and less obvious to others. An extraordinary image, even when pointed out to us, can fade in and out in front of our eyes, such as a Bearded Man on pages

And then there are the 'soft ghosts' which is an expression we use quite often at Ghoststudy. com. This describes a photo anomaly that resembles a human face or figure, vague enough to be an optical illusion. But then again there is just the outside chance that we might be witnessing something paranormal after all. With trick of the light photographs there will always be that element of doubt...is it or isn't it a ghost?

Apparition's Evening Stroll

This picture was taken by ghost enthusiast Stacy using a 35mm camera with 400 speed film. Stacy and the rest of her ghost hunting team had taken thousands of pictures over the course of several months when finally, after all of the hours they had spent in the field and the many pictures they had taken, they were rewarded with this rather remarkable photo of a ghostly figure strolling through a decrepit cemetery in Greenup, Kentucky, USA at around five o'clock on October 28, 2004.

Many are confident that this is a true image of a ghost, however, as always with traditional cameras we have to assure ourselves that double exposure is not the cause of the effect: the negative has been scrutinized by many and it is safe to say that we can rule this out. It appears that there really was something rather creepy roaming the cemetery that day.

'It appears that there really was something rather creepy roaming the cemetery that day...'

Ghost Stuck in Tree

Chad was on his way to pick up his daughter at the child-minder's, as he did everyday, and on this particular day he decided to take a shortcut through the cemetery. He was enjoying the tranquil serenity of his surroundings when something unusual caught his eye – a man lodged within a tree! He immediately rushed to the aid of the trapped man, but as he drew closer to the tree he realized that it was a rather convincing optical illusion. He took several pictures with his digital camera, astonished by what he had found. He even returned later that week to marvel once more at the man stuck in the tree, but imagine his surprise to find that the 'man' had completely disappeared.

Chad says that he was grateful to have had the opportunity to take a picture of such an oddity. Maybe it was just a trick of the light, or maybe the tree had simply decided to swallow the man whole.

'something unusual caught his eye...a man lodged within a tree...'

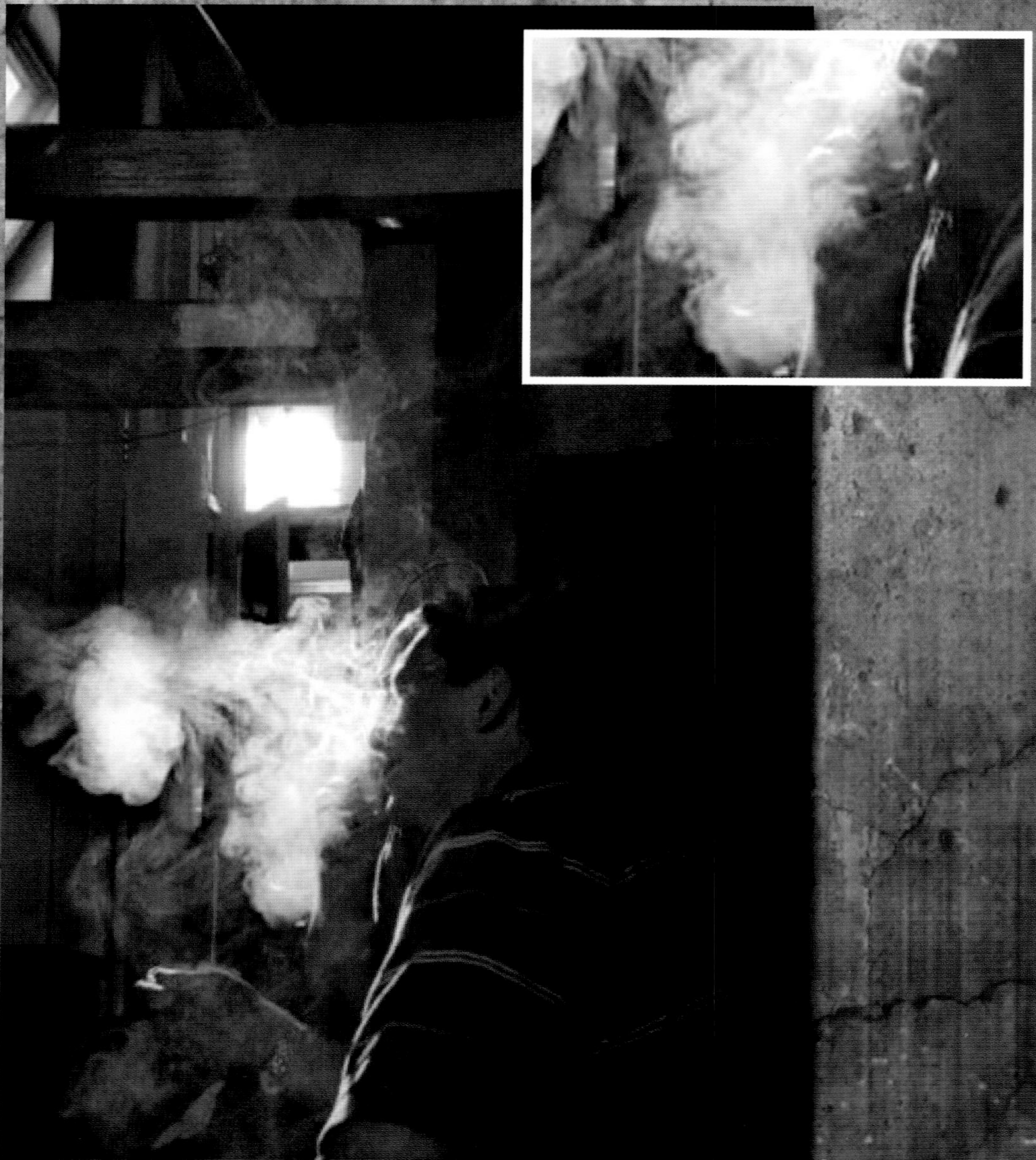

Faces in the Smoke

This photograph was taken by Billy on a holiday with friends in Amsterdam in 2005. They were staying in an attic conversion in a creepy old house. Billy took this picture of his friends Martin and Matty enjoying a cigarette break and, when the photo was developed, he was amazed to see two faces emerge from the smoke. One face is rather vague and is looking towards the smoking men; the other is remarkably clear and appears to be pushing away from the arm of the smoker.

Billy was using a disposable camera which explains why the quality of the picture is so poor, but he cannot explain the appearance of the faces which continue to disturb him to this day. It is quite possible that this illusion is a trick of the light. But we should also consider the possibility that these are supernatural beings making themselves known through the smoke.

'two faces emerge from the smoke, one vague and the other remarkably clear...'

Screaming Ghost

This impressive image of a screaming ghost is unmistakable – you can even see the detail in its eyes, which are particularly compelling. Elizabeth tells us that her house has been in her family for three generations and that her grandfather had died there. Her brother and sister had recently helped her build a new porch at the front of the house, and all was going well until this image appeared on the completed wooden porch.

There's too much detail in and around the face to simply dismiss it, but at the same time we need to consider the fact that the eyes and mouth could actually be knots in the wood and that the shape of the face might be created from the markings and indents made by saw blades, or by the construction wood having been weather-worn. This ghostly apparition is more than likely just a trick of light; either that or her grandfather is trying to show what he thought of his children's efforts at DIY.

'There's too much detail in the face for us to simply dismiss it...'

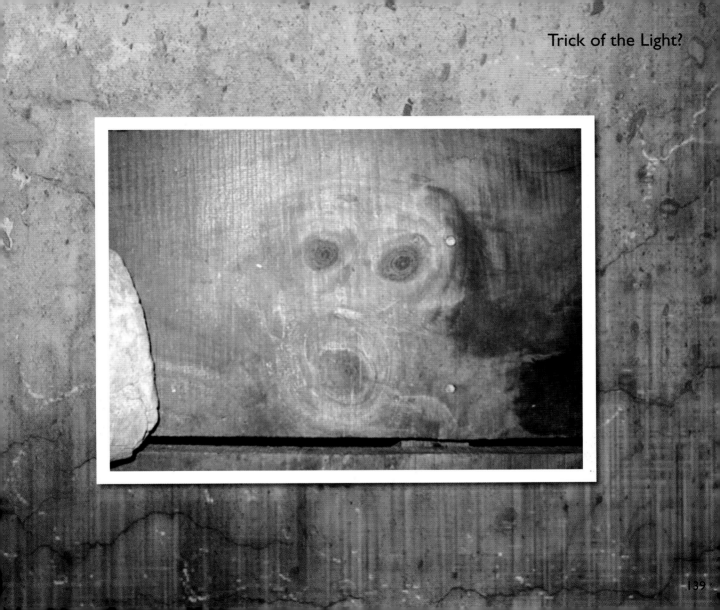

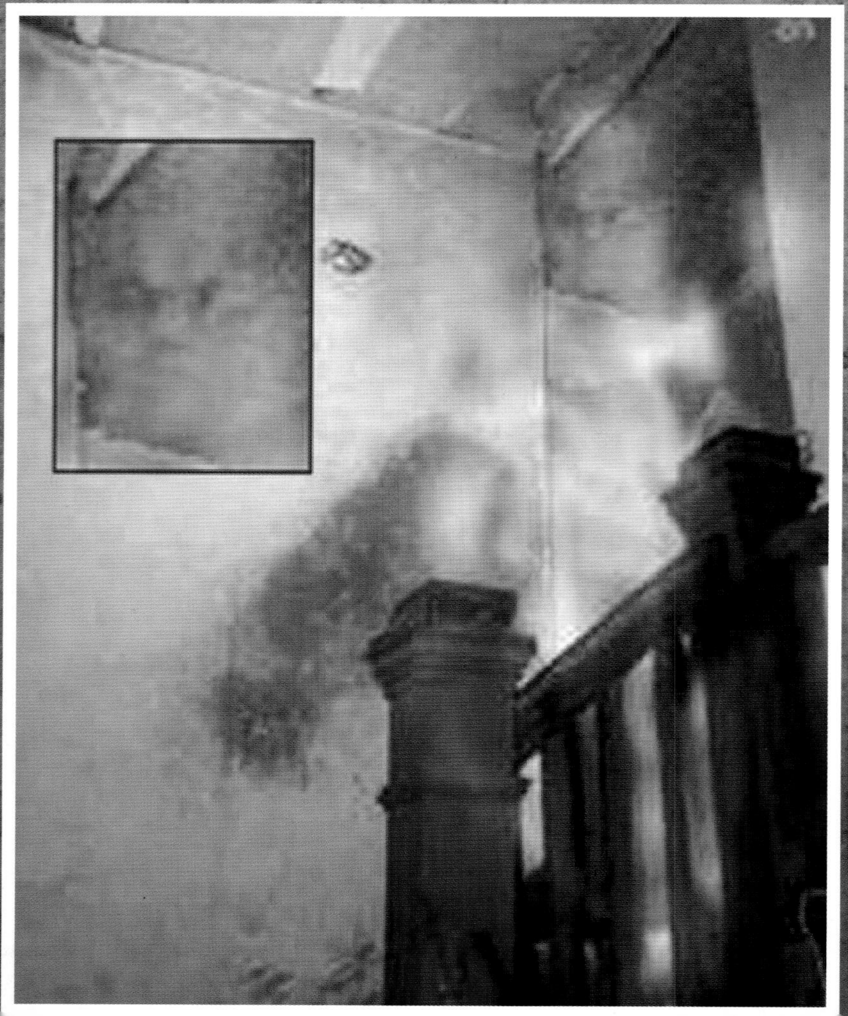

Stairway Apparition

Leonard believes that the image in this photograph is that of his father who had passed away 20 days before. After his father died, Leonard began redecorating the family home and several pictures were taken of the work in progress. One of the developed pictures caught this ghostly image of the face and outline of a man at the top of the stairs. Leonard says that there is no question in his mind that this is his father's ghost and that he looks as grumpy in death as he did in life.

Remodelling a home has a tendency to stir up ghostly activity, and we would be foolish to ignore the passing of Leonard's father just a few days earlier. Although this may be just a trick of the light or glare from the flash causing the white spots, perhaps the ghost of Leonard's father has made an appearance to register his disapproval of the redecorating of his home.

'this is Leonard's father's ghost and he looks as grumpy in death as he did in life...'

Face in the Jeans

If you look closely at this photo you can see an incredibly detailed face in a pair of jeans – even the eyelashes are prominent. Darren took this photo with his mobile phone after he heard a loud noise coming from his bedroom. When he entered the room, he claims to have seen this face on his jeans and so he immediately grabbed his camera to capture it.

Photos like this are often labelled as 'pareidolia', where we see something we want to see rather than what is actually there. A common instance of this is when we perceive a shadow thrown by a piece of furniture in a darkened room as a person. Here the patterns of light and shadow on the jean fabric may have been interpreted as that most familiar of images – the human face. Interestingly, if you look closely, the bag lying next to the jeans also takes on the form of a face.

'he heard a loud noise coming from his bedroom...'

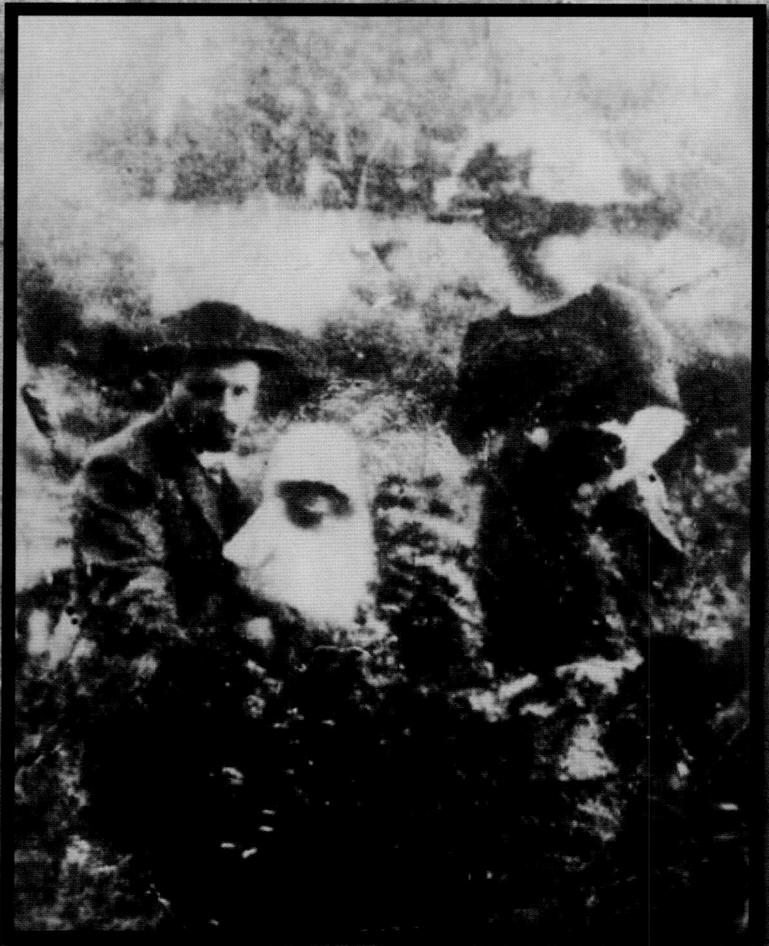

Baby or Bearded Man?

What do you see in this picture – a father, mother and baby on a family outing in the country, or an apparition of Jesus separating the seated man and the standing woman? Some only see a father sitting with a baby on his lap while others see the profile of a bearded man. The baby is wearing a white dress and a large bonnet. But look again and the baby's face becomes a man's eye, the baby's arm his nose, while the grass and bushes around the family group define his hair and beard.

This extraordinary photograph was submitted by Louise who found it among her father's belongings after his death. She believes it dates back to the late 19th century. Although she is aware that it is probably just an optical illusion, she believes it has a spiritual significance for her family.

'Some only see a father sitting with a baby on his lap while others see the profile of a bearded man...'

Cathedral Appears on Wall

A trick of the light photograph of such incredible detail, such magnificent grandeur, this intriguing apparition of a majestic cathedral which appeared on a plastic panel propped up against a wall in an ordinary family home has baffled those who have studied it.

Evaristo took this picture on a sunny morning in 2003. She was visiting her parents and decided to take some photos with her new digital camera before returning home. In the background of this photo of her mother and sister, she was amazed to see the reflection of a grand cathedral creating a particularly fitting backdrop to the family's Last Supper figurine.

It is not known what caused this amazing reflection to appear, but Evaristo describes it as an overwhelming experience for the family.

'an overwhelming experience for the family...'

Alien in Vacuum Cleaner

Steve was so startled by the apparition that appeared in his vacuum cleaner's dust canister following a cleaning session one day that he felt compelled to submit this extraordinary photograph.
At a glance it appears to be an alien that has been sucked into the cylinder.

It is a very convincing depiction of an alien, but this is more than likely just a simple illusion. Lighting, glare, dust and dirt are the most likely culprits. Alien or dust, either way, it is bound to sell for an absolute fortune one day.

'it appears to be an alien that has been sucked into a vacuum cleaner...'

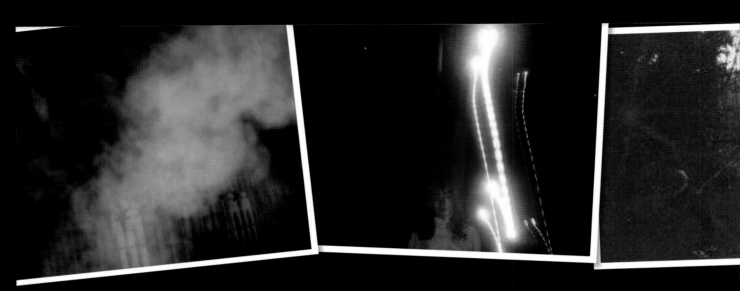

SPOTTING A FAKE

In previous chapters we have covered several categories of ghost photos, so it's only fitting that our final chapter should concentrate on what we like to call 'false positives'.

While there are many fascinating ghost photos around, you can be sure that a large percentage of them are incorrectly identified. Misplaced camera straps, cigarette smoke clouds and a variety of other occurrences are often mistaken for spectral visitations. Most often this is an error of analysis but on occasion there is an intention to mislead – to produce a fake ghost picture.

We'll show you how to diagnose a fake and we'll cover several different types here. It is disappointing that there are individuals who want to discredit paranormal research by producing false images, by fraudulently manipulating a photograph with image software or by tampering with the circumstances in which a photograph is taken, with the intention to deceive.

All the photos presented here are examples that the unquestioning could wrongly analyse, misinterpret or be manipulated by. If we are to advance our knowledge and understanding of

the paranormal world, it is important for us to be as accurate as possible. We need to know how to spot a fake or false image so that we can be sure of ourselves when we do encounter real ghosts on film.

An example of photo manipulation.

(his sister) walked out of the frame. This had the effect of making her look transparent and then Nick was able to create this rather convincing illusion of a ghost. Some websites have even published it as a true apparition. It's one thing to create an illusion but quite another to do it with the intent of deceit. Those who are creating such illusions and passing them off as real are damaging the efforts of the paranormal community to authenticate and substantiate the afterlife.

Breath on Film

This photo was taken at a cemetery in Coloma, California, USA at a family plot that was enclosed with wrought-iron fencing. It was a dark, cold evening – perfect conditions for breath to be visible. Depending on the circumstances,

Photos of breath on film often claim to be ectoplasm.

Photo Manipulation

Photo manipulation is on the rise, especially with the surge of photo imaging software which is available to just about anybody. However, it's not just with software that these types of photos are being created: spraying silly string, placing a dummy or cardboard cutout in a window, camera trickery – the list is endless. The photographer, Nick, is happy to share how he achieved this ghostly image of a woman by simply adjusting his shutter speed. He took the photo with a 60 second exposure and used quick bursts of flash: 30 seconds in, his subject

A convincing optical illusion.

What look like blue spiders are actually electrical discharges.

breath will usually appear blotchy or dense, or sometimes both. The outline of the breath on film will seem smooth and will appear white or grimy brown. Photos that claim to be of ectoplasm are often just breath on a chilly night or cigarette smoke. To avoid this, stretch your camera out in front of you at arms' length, holding your breath and making sure that no one else is standing close by. Breathing within a foot of the lens will have similar effects to the one shown here. Be especially careful if you are out of breath and breathing hard.

Static Spiders

What look like giant blue spiders are actually electrical discharges on the film. This looks very convincing, but it is definitely not a supernatural force. If it's a cold day and you're getting static shocks from the car door or your clothes are sticking to you, this occurrence could happen to your film. Winding your film too fast on days that are high in static electricity will create these 'spiders' on the film of your traditional camera.

Optical Illusions

Ghostly illusions (above left) are often known as simulacra -- an image that has a passing or superficial likeness to the original. In this case, the face on the headstone is nothing more than a stain created by the elements. However, if the image had shown up on film but was not visible to the eye, then we would be considering the likelihood of it being supernatural. Pareidolia is another term which ghost hunters use when they consider the authenticity of a photo. This means that an image is more likely to be an illusion created by our brains wanting to see something rather than something real. Optical illusions are inevitable in the hunt for proof of the paranormal.

Above: Cigarette smoke can be mistaken for ectomist.

Below: Lens flare produces the same effect as orbs.

Cigarette Smoke

In the ghost hunting community, ectoplasm or ectomist is considered to be a form of spiritual energy. It's normally photographed in the form of 'smoky mist' with various shapes and colours. However, cigarette smoke is different as it's usually quite 'stringy' with thick and thin strands. The colours range from white to shades of grey and it is quite easy to spot. As you can see in the picture, the smoke is close to the lens indicating that the photographer was smoking.

Lens Flare

The flash on a shiny object at night can produce some amazing ghostly effects, and lens flare can easily be mistaken for orbs. Needless to say if you face the sun (even indirectly) when taking pictures you are likely to get an effect similar to this picture (left). So stay away from the sun by day and shiny objects by night and you should avoid the effects of lens flare.

Motion Blur

A huge problem for ghost hunters is the common mistake of motion blur. This is particularly common for pictures taken at night. Unless you are using a tripod, you are bound to experience this occurrence; however these days most cameras come with an 'image stabilization' tool which can help to alleviate the effects of motion blur, especially for night-time shots which require a longer exposure time. The photo shown oppisite displays obvious signs of motion blur – the camera had tilted slightly and the light streams are nothing more than a light source outside of the picture, or something reflected from the flash.

Long Exposures

Long exposure photography is an effective tool for creating fraudulent ghost images. This picture (right) was taken with a 35mm camera on a tripod at a very slow shutter speed, while a girl dressed in a white nightgown walked down the stairs past the girl seated on the step. It looks very convincing; however, the giveaway is that the moving girl's foot can be seen in the picture, where she must have paused briefly while passing by. Long-exposure techniques can also be a powerful tool for capturing authentic ghostly activity. Setting a long exposure of 5–10 seconds would not only increase the chances of capturing something supernatural, it would also display a travel pattern and approximate speed. It can be well worth the effort of pulling out the tripod to see what you can capture.

Above and right: Long exposure can produce ghostly effects.

Left: Motion blur is common with pictures taken at night.

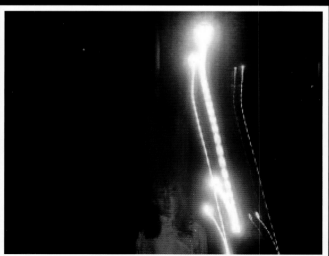

Orbs, (Spirit Globules)

If you own a digital camera you are most likely to see orbs in your photos. From our studies we know that dust and any other airborne particles close to the lens can create 'false positive' orbs. These false anomalies will usually have the appearance of a cell wall and a nucleus. Digital cameras are notorious for creating false positive orbs, but there are ways to spot a fake. If you have multiple orbs in a single photo, then it's probably just dust; or if the orbs have a substance to them then it is probably an uncontrollable occurrence within your camera. Different cameras can create their own unique orb effects. There are many

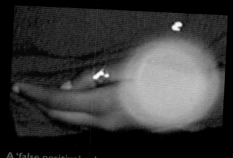

A 'false positive' orb.

If you take a picture in light it produces drizzle orbs.

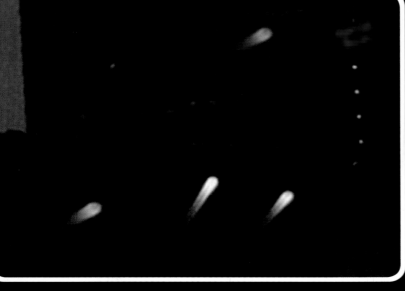

things to consider when it comes to orb photography but the most important thing to remember is that very few orbs are true supernatural beings and there really is no conclusive way to authenticate an orb photo.

Drizzle Orbs

This particular photo (left) displays the phenomena known as 'drizzle orbs' which is an effect caused by the camera. It occurs when pictures are taken in light rain or when there is moisture in the air. The result looks like multiple shooting orbs that appear to be moving in an upwards direction. Drizzle orbs only occur with digital cameras.

Camera-Strap 'Vortex'

A common mistake for ghost hunters is leaving the camera strap on when taking a picture. A camera strap can appear in different forms depending on the flash, settings and the distance from the lens at the time.

Fingers on Film

Most of us have taken photos where a finger shows up in the picture, but sometimes people mistake them for ghosts. Fingers generally show up on the right side of the picture because that's where the shutter release button is normally located. It's not always easy to place fingers firmly when taking a picture but try to hold the camera correctly to avoid pink blob finger shots on your photographs.

01 09 2009 10 29

Above: Try to hold the camera correctly to avoid pink blob finger shots.

Left: A common error is to leave the camera strap in view when taking a picture.

Acknowledgements

Ghost Photography has always been an overwhelming fascination for me. I loved it so much I built a website for viewers to share ghost photos and experiences. So it would seem ungrateful of me if I did not first thank the viewers of Ghoststudy.com for sharing their fascinating photos and experiences. Most of the photos you will see in this book come from the site and they are extraordinary! My family also deserves praise for having had the patience to deal with me during the months of writing this book. It was an interesting time for all of us. I wouldn't have even had the opportunity to write such a book if it weren't for my publishers, Neil and Verity. Neil for trusting me with such a task and then laying out such a precise action plan for me to follow. And Verity for making it all come together in such a remarkable way. Kudos to all of the staff who were involved in this project, from planning to layout and finally publishing! I am of course grateful also to Dr Melvyn Willin for writing book the original adventures in ghost photographs *Ghosts Caught on Film*. He led the way and paved the road for others like myself to follow. And finally, a big hug and special thanks to my good friend and neighbour, Christy Blevins for checking my work and boosting my confidence through this whole process. And last but certainly not least, my supreme gratitude to my Father in Heaven for the abilities, talents and opportunities he has blessed me with.

Picture credits

These images have come from many sources and acknowledgment has been made wherever possible. If images have been used without due credit or acknowledgment, through no fault of our own, apologies are offered. If notified, the publisher will be pleased to rectify any errors or omissions in future editions.

Index